| Fair Trade

Other Books in the Current Controversies Series

Fair Trade

Ariana Agrios, Book Editor

GREENHAVEN
PUBLISHING

Published in 2020 by Greenhaven Publishing, LLC
353 3rd Avenue, Suite 255, New York, NY 10010

Copyright © 2020 by Greenhaven Publishing, LLC

First Edition

Articles in Greenhaven Publishing anthologies are often edited for length to meet page
requirements. In addition, original titles of these works are changed to clearly present
the main thesis and to explicitly indicate the author's opinion. Every effort is made to
ensure that Greenhaven Publishing accurately reflects the original intent of the authors.
Every effort has been made to trace the owners of the copyrighted material.

Cover image: thi/Shutterstock.com

Cataloging-in-Publication Data

Names: Agrios, Ariana, editor.
Title: Fair trade / Ariana Agrios, book editor.
Other titles: Fair trade (2020)
Description: First edition. | New York : Greenhaven Publishing, 2020. | Series: Current
controversies | Includes bibliographical references and index. | Audience: Grades 9-12.
Identifiers: LCCN 2019022598 | ISBN 9781534506091 (library
binding) | ISBN 9781534506084 (paperback)
Subjects: LCSH: International trade—Moral and ethical aspects—Juvenile literature.
| International trade—Environmental aspects—Juvenile literature. | Competition,
Unfair—Juvenile literature. | Developing countries—Commerce—Juvenile literature.
Classification: LCC HF1379 .F3373 2020 | DDC 382/.3091724—dc23
LC record available at https://lccn.loc.gov/2019022598

Manufactured in the United States of America

Website: http://greenhavenpublishing.com

Contents

Chapter 1: Does Fair Trade Support Local Workers and Economies?

Anca Voinea

While some researchers argue that participating in a fair trade cooperative can improve farmers' economic conditions and reduce their exploitation, others found that fair trade did little to improve poverty levels or change working conditions.

Yes: Fair Trade Supports Local Workers and Economies

Sporcle Inc.

Fair trade offers consumers the ability to contribute to equality and fair wage practices through their purchases.

Bob Doherty

By paying farmers a fair price for their labor and products, fair trade seeks to correct growing inequality and food insecurity in developing nations.

Matthias Schmelzer

Though it may not be the most efficient way to assist the global south in economic development, fair trade provides both monetary and non-monetary benefits to producers who participate. This strengthens their power as international traders.

Elen Jones

Through improving access to childcare, health care, and education; promoting higher wages; and helping to fight the impacts of climate change, fair trade works to improve the lives of the impoverished in many ways.

No: Fair Trade Does Not Support Local Workers and Economies

Chapter 2: Does Fair Trade Protect the Environment?

Yes: Fair Trade Protects the Environment

No: Fair Trade Does Not Protect the Environment

Chapter 3: Does Fair Trade Positively Impact Communities?

Fair trade cannot help most poor nations and assists only relatively rich, developing countries due to the high startup fees required for certification.

Chapter 4: Is Fair Trade Actually Fair?

consumers who care about social justice, economic equality, and the environment.

No: Fair Trade Is Not Fair

Foreword

"Controversy" is a word that has an undeniably unpleasant connotation. It carries a definite negative charge. Controversy can spoil family gatherings, spread a chill around classroom and campus discussion, inflame public discourse, open raw civic wounds, and lead to the ouster of public officials. We often feel that controversy is almost akin to bad manners, a rude and shocking eruption of that which must not be spoken or thought of in polite, tightly guarded society. To avoid controversy, to quell controversy, is often seen as a public good, a victory for etiquette, perhaps even a moral or ethical imperative.

Yet the studious, deliberate avoidance of controversy is also a whitewashing, a denial, a death threat to democracy. It is a false sterilizing and sanitizing and superficial ordering of the messy, ragged, chaotic, at times ugly processes by which a healthy democracy identifies and confronts challenges, engages in passionate debate about appropriate approaches and solutions, and arrives at something like a consensus and a broadly accepted and supported way forward. Controversy is the megaphone, the speaker's corner, the public square through which the citizenry finds and uses its voice. Controversy is the life's blood of our democracy and absolutely essential to the vibrant health of our society.

Our present age is certainly no stranger to controversy. We are consumed by fierce debates about technology, privacy, political correctness, poverty, violence, crime and policing, guns, immigration, civil and human rights, terrorism, militarism, environmental protection, and gender and racial equality. Loudly competing voices are raised every day, shouting opposing opinions, putting forth competing agendas, and summoning starkly different visions of a utopian or dystopian future. Often these voices attempt to shout the others down; there is precious little listening and considering among the cacophonous din. Yet listening and considering, too, are essential to the health of a democracy. If controversy is democracy's lusty lifeblood, respectful listening and careful thought are its higher faculties, its brain, its conscience.

Current Controversies does not shy away from or attempt to hush the loudly competing voices. It seeks to provide readers with as wide and representative as possible a range of articulate voices on any given controversy of the day, separates each one out to allow it to be heard clearly and fairly, and encourages careful listening to each of these well-crafted, thoughtfully expressed opinions, supplied by some of today's leading academics, thinkers, analysts, politicians, policy makers, economists, activists, change agents, and advocates. Only after listening to a wide range of opinions on an issue, evaluating the strengths and weaknesses of each argument, assessing how well the facts and available evidence mesh with the stated opinions and conclusions, and thoughtfully and critically examining one's own beliefs and conscience can the reader begin to arrive at his or her own conclusions and articulate his or her own stance on the spotlighted controversy.

This process is facilitated and supported in each Current Controversies volume by an introduction and chapter overviews that provide readers with the essential context they need to begin engaging with the spotlighted controversies, with the debates surrounding them, and with their own perhaps shifting or nascent opinions on them. Chapters are organized around several key questions that are answered with diverse opinions representing all points on the political spectrum. In its content, organization, and methodology, readers are encouraged to determine the authors' point of view and purpose, interrogate and analyze the various arguments and their rhetoric and structure, evaluate the arguments' strengths and weaknesses, test their claims against available facts and evidence, judge the validity of the reasoning, and bring into clearer, sharper focus the reader's own beliefs and conclusions and how they may differ from or align with those in the collection or those of classmates.

Research has shown that reading comprehension skills improve dramatically when students are provided with compelling, intriguing, and relevant "discussable" texts. The subject matter of these collections could not be more compelling, intriguing, or urgently relevant to today's students and the world they are poised to inherit. The anthologized articles also provide the basis for stimulating, lively, and passionate classroom debates. Students who are compelled to anticipate objections to their own argument and identify the flaws in those of an opponent read more carefully, think more critically, and steep themselves in relevant context, facts, and information more thoroughly. In short, using discussable text of the kind provided by every single volume in the Current Controversies series encourages close reading, facilitates reading comprehension, fosters research, strengthens critical thinking, and greatly enlivens and energizes classroom discussion and participation. The entire learning process is deepened, extended, and strengthened.

If we are to foster a knowledgeable, responsible, active, and engaged citizenry, we must provide readers with the intellectual, interpretive, and critical-thinking tools and experience necessary to make sense of the world around them and of the all-important debates and arguments that inform it. We must encourage them not to run away from or attempt to quell controversy but to embrace it in a responsible, conscientious, and thoughtful way, to sharpen and strengthen their own informed opinions by listening to and critically analyzing those of others. This series encourages respectful engagement with and analysis of current controversies and competing opinions and fosters a resulting increase in the strength and rigor of one's own opinions and stances. As such, it helps readers assume their rightful place in the public square and provides them with the skills necessary to uphold their awesome responsibility—guaranteeing the continued and future health of a vital, vibrant, and free democracy.

Introduction

> *"Fair Trade is complicated. And as with any system, there are those who find ways to take advantage, so in some instances the benefits may not trickle down to the workers as intended ... [But] while there may be more examples of this type of abuse, it is by no means conclusive that the practice of Fair Trade overall does not work."*
>
> *–Amy Shoenthal, journalist*

Trade is the act of buying and selling goods and services. In today's globalized world that often occurs in an international context. Over the last several decades trade relations around the world have grown more complicated and have distanced buyers from sellers. In the 1960s, several organizations became concerned about rising poverty rates in developing countries as a direct impact of international trade. In response, they created the fair trade movement.

"Fair trade" is simply defined as trade that pays sellers a fair price for the goods they produce. Over time the small organizations that promoted fair trade for their own products came together and formed the formal fair trade organizations known around the world today. Though several organizations exist that promote fair trade, the most well known and established is Fairtrade International. They, like other organizations, set a strict set of standards that producers must abide by in order to qualify their product as fair trade. These include labor and environmental standards that ensure fair pay, safe working conditions, better practices for the environment, and more.

If a product carries the fair trade symbol, then a fair trade organization has verified that the workers who produced and sold the product made an equitable wage for their work and have abided by the standards set by the organization. This acts as a signal for consumers and shows that the product they are purchasing was created without any exploitation of workers. However, opponents of fair trade believe these standards often go unenforced and that exploitation can continue to occur.

Fair trade participants include produce farmers, coffee and chocolate producers, and even clothes and textiles vendors. These fair trade producers live on nearly every continent, though fair trade organizations work primarily with producers in Central and South America, Africa, and South Asia. Fair trade consumers are simply anyone who chooses to buy fair trade certified products in stores. As one might assume, fair trade producers come from typically poorer countries, while fair trade consumers live in wealthier nations. This is because the fair trade movement originated to help the poorest and most disadvantaged in the global trading network.

Two of the unique factors of fair trade that distinguish it from other international trade are the fair trade minimum and the fair trade premium. A fair trade minimum is simply a price floor—meaning the lowest acceptable price—which employers must meet when paying their workers. This minimum set by fair trade organizations is designed to raise wages and reduce poverty. Companies in poverty-stricken regions often take advantage of the low wages they can pay workers who will accept low pay over the possibility of no income. Fair trade seeks to minimize this exploitation.

The fair trade premium is perhaps the most distinct feature of fair trade. The premium is an additional price levied on producers of fair trade products that must be put towards community projects. This can range from social projects that help increase access to education to environmental projects that assist with forest regeneration and carbon emission reduction. Workers within each company decide how to spend this premium based on the needs of their communities. However, critics of fair trade believe these premiums fail to address real problems. They argue these premiums don't reach those who are most in need of help and that fair trade standards lack enough definition to truly ensure sustainable and just practices.

But how do producers become fair trade certified and cover these additional costs? To participate as a fair trade certified organization, companies must pay a fee to the fair trade foundation with whom they decide to work. Unfortunately, critics believe these upfront costs cause an unfair barrier to entry that prevents the producers most in need of fair trade from becoming certified and reaping the associated benefits. These fees cover the necessary monitoring costs to ensure fair trade organizations are adhering to the required standards. To cover the additional costs of the minimum and premium, fair trade products impose a higher price on consumers than alternative goods. Differences in prices range greatly, as there is no formula for setting fair trade final product prices. Each producing company arranges a price with individual vendors that choose to sell fair trade goods.

Fair trade products are available in countries around the world, but their popularity varies greatly across nations. The United Kingdom and Australia have long been supporters of fair trade products, and these products are more commonly available in their grocery stores. The popularity of fair trade products in the United States varies by region, but they are generally less widely available as an alternative to regular products than in Australia and the United Kingdom. One might have seen the fair trade certification label, but only on coffee products, or maybe never at all.

So, if fair trade is better for workers, communities, and the environment, why is it not the only form of trade we accept? Some argue that fair trade might not live up to all its hype. Some researchers believe that the premium doesn't reach the community it's designed to help, while others believe the fair trade minimum might actually keep workers in poverty rather than help them out of it. Fair trade also breaks basic economic rules in setting prices and supply above the equilibriums demanded by the market. *Current Controversies: Fair Trade* works through the literature and debate on the economic, environmental, and social benefits of fair trade and asks readers to consider whether fair trade is truly fair.

Does Fair Trade Support Local Workers and Economies?

Fair Trade and Worker Exploitation

Anca Voinea

Anca Voinea is a journalist and international editor at Co-op News.

This year's Fairtrade Fortnight is themed around fighting the exploitation of small-scale farmers. But what about the workers employed by these farmers and other larger producers?

Finding Exploitation in Your Supply Chain

One of the risks behind the Fairtrade label can be the treatment of workers employed by producers: whether they are working for a large co-operative or a smallholder farmer, the rights of these "wage workers" can go unnoticed.

The treatment of these workers is taken into account for Fairtrade certification, but it's difficult to police, says Dr Carlos Oya, a lecturer in political economy at SOAS University of London, who has researched the issue in Ethiopia and Uganda. He found that people employed by smallholder farmers were not being monitored and that Fairtrade did not have a positive (or negative) effect on their wages or working conditions.

"The problem is the assumption that small producer organisations are producers only—so the certification only applies to producers ... the people missed out completely are casual and seasonal workers who work for smallholder producers," says Dr Oya.

"Fairtrade's response is that it is impossible to monitor, and we agree, it's really difficult—but that doesn't remove the problem."

A study by the United States Agency for International Development (USAID) also discovered that Fairtrade is highly ineffective in reaching those who depend on a wage through agricultural labour.

"How Is Fairtrade Tackling the Problem of Worker Exploitation?" by Anca Voinea, Co-operative Press Ltd (www.thenews.coop), February 2, 2017. Reprinted by permission.

What Is Fairtrade Doing?

The issue of exploitation fits in with the theme of this year's Fairtrade Fortnight, which is fighting the exploitation of small-scale farmers. There are over 1.4 million farmers and 204,000 workers spread across more than 74 countries participating in Fairtrade.

What does the Fairtrade Foundation mean when it talks about addressing exploitation? Adam Gardner, communities campaign manager, explains: "The food on our tables, the tea and coffee in our mugs, all come from farmers who work hard but are not paid what they deserve.

"Whether in the UK or in Malawi, no one deserves to be short-changed for a hard day's work. When we reach for the cheapest products, we may be unconsciously feeding exploitation. We become part of the problem, but we can make a conscious choice to be part of the solution and support trade that is fair."

Fairtrade's revised standards for hired labour, which came into effect in 2015, said that all workers must be on the Fairtrade Premium Committee, which is responsible for the management of the Fairtrade Premium.

In addition, they have the right to join an independent union to collectively negotiate their working conditions. Another criterion is that salaries must be equal or higher than the regional average or than the minimum wage in effect.

In 2016, Fairtrade, together with the Global Living Wage Coalition, published a number of living wage benchmarks.

The organisation also provides additional training initiatives and multi-stakeholder dialogues to form consensus on the measures needed to close the gap between living wage level and current wages from an industry point of view and with groups on the ground.

The Issue of Hired Labour

Many Fairtrade producers, such as those producing coffee, have fixed seasons and require temporary workers. Wilbert Flinterman, senior advisor on Workers' Rights at Fairtrade International, says this is a challenge and the organisation works closely with farmers in many ways.

"In terms of standards we say that employers have to ensure that wages and benefits are similar for permanent and seasonal workers," he says.

"It's clearly more challenging to verify compliance of contractors but that's what we expect of operators. Many farmers certified are to an extent operating in the informal sector, where they are not receiving social benefits. They are small producers so that impacts on our ability to collect information from them."

Mr Flinterman added: "Our aim is improve the economic justice in the value chain so that farmers are able to gain income and support workers. Our focus is to help farmers make the transition from formal to informal sector in such a way that is economically sustainable for them.

"For example, we provide training to banana farmers on HR practices so that they gain skills and knowledge to provide better employment conditions to workers and put policies and procedures in place."

Fairtrade International also ran an HR training programme in Peru in 2014 that will be rolled out in other countries in Latin America. According to Mr Flinterman, the project was a "significant success judging from the feedback."

He added: "We worked with local people, strongly supported by producers themselves. We developed training in such a way that is relevant to smallholder farmers. We helped them to set up a very basic database for personnel administration, policies and procedures, dispute resolution, informing farmers about workers' rights and occupation health and safety. This all works toward the objective of treating people equally.

"We have to make sure that Fairtrade is accessible to smallholder farmers, so that thresholds to enter Fairtrade and benefit from instruments, support services and market access provided by Fairtrade are not too high and we have to understand that after certification we still have to work with farmers in the process of development.''

A Problem of Context?

London University's Dr Carlos Oya says that alongside the labour monitoring issues, a problem is the existing context in each country and the specific characteristics of smallholder producer organisations.

"Despite interventions of Fairtrade and other certification systems, a lot of the dynamics of these producer organisations cannot be changed rapidly—the power inequality in them is very hard to tackle," he says.

Dr Oya says the reporting mechanisms of these certification systems are not enough to alter those conditions. "Yes, a co-op can give evidence of assembly with members, where they make decisions democratically about using premiums, but that is a formality, are they actually working democratically?

"The fact these members in co-ops have greater power than others, shape what others think, is a very important aspect of this project. Producer organisations are complex, there are a lot of power relations in them and a system of formalities in auditing doesn't necessarily alter the system of power, most members inactive, the ones who call the shots are in the headquarters of the co-op."

Dr Oya pointed out that in the region covered by his research, co-operatives tend to have been set up by the government as a way for state to organise distribution.

"The notion of co-operative is stretched to any collective of producers who share some infrastructure for marketing purposes," he adds.

"It is not possible to say co-ops are better because the boundaries are blurred. It is difficult to know if it is a co-op or normal producer organisation."

But he welcomed the work done by Fairtrade in collaboration with other organisations on as part of the Global Living Wage coalition. He added that setting out living wage standards for different countries would require a lot of research.

Supply Chain Involvement

Stirling Smith, who has worked as a consultant with the ILO, Fair Labour Association, Ethical Trading Initiative, trade unions, NGOs and the Co-operative College, says the potential of trade between co-ops to help ensure a fairer supply chain was often neglected.

He believes co-ops should consciously ask themselves how they can reshape the supply chain and seek to find co-operative suppliers for the products they need. He gave the example of FinTea, a Fairtrade project involving 11,000 Kenyan tea farmers.

After receiving the Fairtrade certification, FinTea Growers made its way to the shelves, becoming part of the Co-operative Group's iconic 99 Fairtrade Tea in the UK.

The Co-operative College designed the training to help the farmers to establish their own co-operatives, in collaboration with the Co-operative College of Kenya. The Co-operative Group co-funded the project and is buying from the producers.

"It's an interesting example because if you look at the increase of income for those tea farmers, it was cutting out the middleman rather than the Fairtrade Premium that really helped them. They sold to the co-op and kept the margin."

Simel Esim, chief of the ILO's Cooperatives Unit also believes co-ops have a part to play in the supply chain: "Unleashing the potential of co-operatives for fair trade is something that needs to be on the national, regional, international policy makers' agendas," she says.

"And at the same time, co-operatives need to do more to—and do better at—improving their labour and environmental practices toward a more sustainable future."

Fairtrade Groups

- Fairtrade Labelling Organizations International (FLO International, or Fairtrade International): Established 1997.

An association of 3 producer networks, 19 national labelling initiatives and 3 marketing organizations that promote and market the Fairtrade Certification Mark in their countries.

- Fairtrade Foundation: Established 1992. The British member of FLO International. An independent charity that licenses use of the Fairtrade Mark on products in the UK in accordance with internationally agreed standards.

What Does the Research Say?

- A 2013 study by researchers at the University of Göttingen found that Fairtrade certification cuts the likelihood of being poor by 50% in Uganda—but the impacts of standards and certification systems largely depend on many factors at local level.
- A study by LEI Wageningen (commissioned by Fairtrade International) found that Fairtrade workers feel more empowered than their non-FT counterparts, though no strong differences are found for all empowerment issues. However, the report could not conclude whether overall working conditions (in terms of worker rights) on Fairtrade-certified plantations were better than non-certified plantations.
- USAID research suggests a key issue to consider over the effects of Fairtrade is the assumption that rural poverty is mainly a problem for smallholder farmers rather than wage-workers employed by producers. Wage work is included in certification standards, but the research said Fairtrade has been shown to be highly ineffective in reaching the poorest members of the respective communities. The USAID report warned: "Simply raising farm gate prices does not automatically raise wages or improve working conditions, and as a result a well-intentioned initiative such as Fairtrade has failed to improve the lives of the poorest people in rural communities."

- Another recent study on Fair Trade, Employment, and Poverty Reduction (FTEPR) in Ethiopia and Uganda assessed Fairtrade's effects on wageworkers and employment. The research compared rural areas dominated by Fairtrade-certified producers with areas where Fairtrade is absent, focusing on coffee, tea, and flower production. The findings confirmed that households that are engaged in agricultural wage labour are likely to be among the poorest in their communities. In addition, the study argued that Fairtrade certification had no statistically significant positive effect on the working conditions of manual agricultural wageworkers.

What Can Co-Operatives Do?

Employers with a turnover in excess of £36m are obligated under the Modern Slavery Act 2015 to eradicate modern slavery in their business and supply chain. But what else can co-operatives do?

- Voluntarily adopt an anti-slavery statement and carry out their own investigations into the supply chain. Wholefood co-operative Suma, for example, ensures producers are compliant with the Ethical Trading Initiative Base Code, which dictates, among other things, that working conditions are safe, child labour is not used and that living wages are paid. In helping to eradicate modern slavery it asks suppliers to complete ethical questionnaires to ensure there is no slavery or trafficking in the supply chain.
- Create your own statement: Co-operatives UK has designed a series of resources, including an anti-slavery statement template, to get co-ops started, which is available online at s.coop/modernslavery.

The Benefits of Fair Trade from the Consumer Perspective

Sporcle Inc.

Sporcle is a trivia website and designer of many popular trivia- and information-based games.

I t's likely you have seen or heard about fair trade products, but have you ever wondered what exactly fair trade means? In this post, we'll look at the question—what is fair trade? We'll also explore some of the benefits of fair trade, and why it is important today.

Knowing Your Food

How consumers shop for and consume food has changed in the past decade, and more and more people want to know where their food is coming from, how it's processed, and what kind of impact it will have on them, their family, and the world.

Knowing the history of your food isn't a bad thing, and this desire has led to other evolutions in agriculture, including changing practices so that fewer chemicals are used on crops and given to livestock, which is healthier for humanity and the environment. More sustainable crop growing practices have also been developed, which benefits humanity now and in the future.

What Is Fair Trade?

While it is important to make sure consumers and the environment are healthy when it comes to growing crops and raising livestock, it's also important that the farmers and the workers are also treated fairly. Farming and livestock raising are a way of life for a multitude of people around the world, but when unfair trade practices exist, it's harder for smaller farms or farmers in poor countries to make

"What Is Fair Trade? | What Are the Benefits of Fair Trade?" Sporcle, Inc., September 29, 2018. Reprinted by permission.

a livable wage from the sale of their goods—assuming they have the opportunity to even sell their goods at the market.

Large corporations that exist in wealthy countries have cornered the agricultural market, making it difficult for smaller or family run farms to sell their goods. This can keep these farmers or the countries they are from in poverty while the bigger companies in the richer countries continue to see profits. Fair trade was developed so that these small producers had equal opportunity to get their products to consumers. Crops and products that are most often impacted by fair trade include sugar, cocoa, tea, coffee, and bananas.

What It Takes to Be Classified Fair Trade

To be a Fair Trade Certified good, there are very specific and rigorous standards that have to be met, including economic, social, and environmental standards. Workers who are instrumental in developing these goods have to have safe work conditions, protect the environment, develop sustainable livelihoods, and ensure that additional funds are invested locally to uplift and empower the communities.

In most cases, Fair Trade Certified products have a "floor" price, which means that crops can't be sold beneath a fixed price, no matter what the market conditions are. The purpose of this is to keep small farms and underrepresented communities safe from market fluctuations, which could ruin their profits. It also protects these farms and communities from being bought out by corporations or larger farms.

What Are the Benefits of Buying Fair Trade Goods?

Buying Fair Trade goods is beneficial to everyone. For consumers, it gives them the opportunity to help out communities and farmers in need. It also encourages and stresses the importance of social change, along with promoting an equitable and just global trading system. When a consumer buys a Fair Trade good, it improves the lives of the farmer and/or the community who produced it.

For companies who carry products produced under Fair Trade, having the label on their goods means that they are credible and want to have a positive impact on the world. Customers probably view them as trustworthy and will happily buy products from them, knowing the purchase is going to a greater good.

Producers who develop Fair Trade goods probably see the most benefit, and they include the following:

- Stable prices—allowing for the costs of sustainable production to be covered
- Market access—allowing producers to find buyers that they wouldn't normally be able to interact with
- Partnerships—producers have the opportunity to make decisions about what will happen to them in the future
- Empowerment—both farmers and workers have the opportunity to develop knowledge, resources, and skills about their trade that will give them more control and power over their lives

Products that have been Fair Trade Certified will carry a seal. If you want to make a difference in the lives of people around the world, look for that symbol on a variety of products available from different sources.

Fair Trade Benefits for the Producer: Ensuring Food Security

Bob Doherty

Bob Doherty is a professor of marketing at the University of York in the United Kingdom and a principal researcher on food resilience programs for the Global Food Security Fund.

Paradoxically, of the one billion people classified as food insecure by the United Nations, about 500 million are smallholder farmers in developing economies. Some of these producers are exporting luxuries such as coffee, cocoa, exotic fruits and sugar for consumers in developed economies. Due to poor and volatile prices coupled with unfair trade rules, they simply don't earn enough to feed their families all year round and often experience the problem of seasonal hunger between harvests.

This lack of nourishment can lead to stunting, weakened immune systems and more vulnerability to disease and infection. Children are particularly vulnerable, as periods of under-nutrition can hinder both their physical and mental development. Seasonal hunger is a serious problem for many coffee and cocoa farmers. Smallholder coffee farmers in three Central American countries were found to have no guarantee of food security for three to four months every year.

Fairtrade was set up initially to work with marginalised smallholder farmers as "a trading partnership, based on dialogue, transparency and respect that seeks greater equity in international trade."

Sales of Fairtrade products have grown to €7.3 billion (£6.3 billion) working with 1,230 producer organisations consisting of 1.6m farmers. Fairtrade certification actively

"Food Security: How Fairtrade Helps Level the Playing Field for Small Producers," by Bob Doherty, The Conversation, January 23, 2017. https://theconversation.com/food-security-how-fairtrade-helps-level-the-playing-field-for-small-producers-70937. Licensed under CC BY 4.0 International.

supports producers in developing countries through importing and retailing their products. Moreover, acting as a social movement, fair trade campaigns for changes in the conventional terms and conditions of international trade which disadvantage producers in developing economies.

The movement prioritises socioeconomic factors by working to facilitate market access for producers, paying producers a fair minimum price which provides producers a guaranteed price when the world market price falls below this level. The stability of the Fairtrade minimum price means that producer cooperatives may be able to obtain finances and credit services. Cooperatives also gain security from longer-term contracts with exporters through the Fairtrade market.

Social Premium

In addition, whatever the conventional market price, producers in the Fairtrade system are also paid a social premium per tonne of produce (for cocoa it is US$200 per tonne) which is used for community infrastructure projects such as crop diversification schemes to combine cash and food crops, building schools, water provision and health services.

Jane Sepkazi, 36, a member of the Sireet OEP tea co-operative in Kenya, is one of the farmers who have been trained by their Fairtrade partners to grow different crops as part of her organisation's plan to increase food security for farmers. The idea is to make farmers less reliant on tea for their income and offer ways to use their land to produce food. Sepkazi lives on her 0.2-hectare farm with her parents and two children and as well as tea, she has chickens and a kitchen garden. "I've been taught poultry keeping so I don't rely just on my tea crop," she said.

The impact of Fairtrade is significant. A study by the Center for Evaluation at Saarland University in Germany found that smallholder farmers who benefited from Fairtrade enjoyed higher and more stable incomes than producers in the respective comparison groups. A further study involving coffee farmers in

Uganda showed that participation in Fairtrade increased household living standards by 30% and significantly reduced the prevalence and depth of poverty.

Banana farmer Julio Mercado Cantillo, 57, lives on his farm in Macondo, Colombia, with his wife Alicia, children and grandchildren. For Cantillo, one of the benefits of Fairtrade has been better and more stable prices for his bananas, which has improved his income and the food security of his family. Cantillo explains:

> When we began growing bananas, it was tough. There were some days when we only had one meal. Since we joined Fairtrade, everything has changed. We now have all of our daily meals and we have also managed from the extra income from Fairtrade to buy farm animals which provides an extra source of food, and the opportunity to bring in more income by selling the animals.

Nicaragua is the second poorest country in Latin America after Haiti and during the "thin season" before the coffee harvest, farmers in central Nicaragua often rely on food programmes to feed their children. To tackle this, the COOMPROCOM coffee cooperative has invested its Fairtrade Premium income in programmes that focus on food and nutritional security in the community. These include setting up a revolving fund that allows farmers to access quick loans to make emergency purchases of food. Another is a programme focusing on child nutrition that encourages farmers to grow food crops (such as beans, rice, tomatoes and corn) and diversify diets so that they are less reliant on food purchases.

Growing Network

To help tackle the problem of seasonal hunger, the Fairtrade movement has also given birth to some very interesting financial institutions such as Shared Interest, Oikocredit and Cordiad which provide social finance for innovative trade mechanisms for smallholder farmer groups such as pre-finance for individual orders, credits and loans for stock facilities and pre-harvest loans when cash flow is a major problem for producers.

Being part of the Fairtrade system provides a very useful safety net for smallholder farmers, but it can't do everything in isolation. Fairtrade works best when it operates as part of a bigger system—within a framework of collaboration backed by supportive policy at national and local level and coupled with meaningful commitments from business.

There is still much work to be done to continue the positive impact of Fairtrade—the movement needs to keep the pressure on both policy makers and business leaders to ensure consumers can choose Fairtrade at the point of purchase. In the UK, Fairtrade companies are having to fight hard to maintain their position on the supermarket shelf—and the movement needs to redouble its efforts to communicate with consumers to explain how their purchase of Fairtrade goods can help people like Sepkazi and the Cantillo family keep their heads above water even when times are tough.

Price Premiums and New Opportunities Benefit Fair Trade Producers and Workers

Matthias Schmelzer

Matthias Schmelzer is a postdoctoral researcher of economic history who has taught at several European universities. He is also an award-winning author for his work on economic growth.

[...]

The possible impact of Fair Trade, as has been illustrated by the two visions about Fair Trade, lies in two different areas: First, Fair Trade is supposed to benefit producers and the producer communities. This is more or less straightforward and uncontroversial and the results of different case studies will be summarized and systematized in the following section. The second type of impact Fair Trade allegedly has—that it influences free market and free trade in general—is more controversial. In order to analyse this claim I will divide it up in three areas. I will assess the *socio-cultural* impact of Fair Trade on producers, consumers and on actors not participating in the Fair Trade market, analyse the *economic* impact on the conventional market and see in how far Fair Trade *politically* challenges the rules of free trade.

Impact on Producers

Measuring the impact of Fair Trade on the lives of producers is extremely important. Fair Trade claims to be an effective way of improving the living standard of producers in the global south, and consumers buy Fair Trade products in the belief that their purchase is having this developmental effect. In the end all the money that NGOs, government agencies and private donators give in support

"In or Against the Market: Is Fair Trade a Neoliberal Solution to Market Failures or a Practical Challenge to Neoliberal Trade and the Free Market Regime in General?" by Matthias Schmelzer, Threefolding. Reprinted by permission.

of Fair Trade and all the money that consumers of Fair Trade products spend on the higher prices of these products could be spent on other development projects that might be more effective.

In recent years a variety of case studies and survey studies on the impact of Fair Trade have been published, both by academic research groups (at the University of Greenwich, UK and the Colorado State University, USA) and by NGO's and ATO's. These studies, most of which are qualitative non-systematic analysis, converge on several general points: Fair Trade has a positive impact on the lives of producers; Fair Trade benefits the producers in a variety of ways beyond increasing income; and the most pervasive problem is that Fair Trade products make up only a part of the sales of producers.

There are some limitations to these impact studies, the most important being that most studies do not compare the changes in incomes and livelihoods of the Fair Trade producers to non-Fair Trade producers and communities and that it is analytically hard to separate the unique contribution of Fair Trade from other influences, especially since Fair Trade projects are often supported in various ways by development agencies.[1] As has been convincingly argued by a survey study of the United Nations Food and Agriculture Organization (FAO), the benefits from developmental aid and from participating in Fair Trade are highly mutually supportive and interlinked. Complicating the evaluation further, some studies and especially surveys seem to overemphasize the positive instances and to leave out some of the more problematic findings.[2]

There are a variety of different impacts on producers. The direct impacts include an increase in income due to the Fair Trade minimum price and the social premium; access to credit; improved education; psychological and organizational effects such as producer empowerment and its effect on civic participation. I will first analyze the benefits from the price premium and other directly financial benefits, I will then assess the non-monetary benefits and the organizational and political impacts of Fair Trade on producers and finally I will try to give a picture of how effective Fair Trade is in transferring money from consumers to producers.

Benefits from the Price Premium

Fair Trade producers receive for their products a floor price, which is, depending on the fluctuations of the world market prices, significantly higher than what conventional buyers pay and an additional social premium. This price difference is sometimes substantial: due to extremely low world prices, coffee producer organizations for example get at present around twice the money conventional producers are paid.

On an aggregate level the direct benefits of this extra income for producers are impressive: This extra income—calculated from the difference of Fair Trade floor prices and world prices for all the certified global retail sales (estimated at US$ 1 billion for 2004) and the social premium—amounted in 2004 to US$100 million, so the 2004-2005 annual report of the FLO. And similarly, the extra benefits for coffee farmers during 2003 amount to over US$22 million, if one calculates the difference between the world market price as defined for Arabica by the New York and for Robusta by the London stock exchange with the Fair Trade minimum price and premium (FLO, 2006).[3] All these benefits are distributed among the 531 producer organizations that are certified by the FLO, representing over one million farmers and workers and, including their families, five million people are affected by the extra income earned through Fair Trade sales above world prices (FLO, 2006). Just looking at these aggregate numbers this means that in 2004 out of US$100 billion consumers spent on Fair Trade products an extra income of almost US$100 on average was transferred to more than one million farmers.

On the micro level the picture is, however, more complex. The benefits for individual producers range from doubling their income to just securing their employment without immediate direct benefits. All studies and surveys conclude that Fair Trade has a positive influence on the income of cooperatives and individual producers, significantly improving their standard of living.[4] Different studies demonstrate however highly differing results even in terms of the basic financial benefits. This reflects the different particular circumstances of producers and their environment as well as the uneven distribution of Fair Trade benefits among the producers organizations.

[...]

In addition to the direct monetary benefits from the Fair Trade price premium another important benefit is the provision of credit at reasonable rates and the pre-financing of up to 60 percent of the price of the purchases, if the cooperative demands that. The provision of credit and prepayment is immensely important and is mentioned in most studies as very positive. A problem that has been reported however is that—contrary to the rules of the different Fair Trade labelling organizations and ATOs—the actual payment comes very late, creating immense financial pressures for producers. In a cooperative in El Salvador farmers complained that the payments were usually delayed by more than 3 months, as opposed to payments after 30 days on the conventional market.

The most pervasive problem and at the same time the major explanation for the difference in the direct benefits for individual producers and cooperatives is that many Fair Trade producer organizations are only able to sell a small portion of their products on the Fair Trade market. The supply by far outstretches the demand. On a world-wide average Fair Trade producers are only able to sell around 42 percent of their product on the Fair Trade market, while Fair Trade coffee cooperatives are selling half of their crops at Fair Trade prices. How this plays out at an individual level is illustrated by a recent study of Nicaraguan coffee farmers. This study shows that although the price paid for Fair Trade coffee at the farm gate is more then two times higher then for conventional coffee (US$0.84/lb as opposed to US$0.39/lb to an agro export company or US$0.37/lb to a local middleman), the average price for all the coffee that Fair Trade farmers get is still very low, only slightly higher than conventional prices and sometimes lower than the monetary production costs (US$0.56/lb as opposed to the conventional average of US$0.40/lb, while the monetary production costs average US$0.49 to 0.79/lb).

[...]

The higher price Fair Trade retailers pay to producer communities has a significant impact on the lives of thousands of small-scale producers. A closer look at different Fair Trade farms and cooperatives shows however that the impact is very different depending on a variety of factors. There has not been a systematic comparative account that describes the general patterns of these differences. But all studies point out that the biggest problem for producer communities is that they cannot sell all their products on the Fair Trade market. The fact that most producer groups in different studies emphasize the need to increase the Fair Trade market furthermore reveals the importance participation in and benefits of Fair Trade has for small-scale producers.

Non-Monetary Benefits

Producers not only directly benefits from the extra income or Fair Trade, but also from long-term relationships, improved organization and market information, all of which may affect their non-Fair Trade relations. In several studies psychological benefits like improved self esteem and pride in the higher level of control over the value chain are evaluated as very beneficial and important. Murray et al for example reports from seven case studies with coffee farmers in Latin America that "in case after case, farmers reported that the increased attention to their farming – including the visits of Fair Trade and organic inspectors, buyers and even visiting Northern consumers (...) promoted renewed pride in coffee farming." Taylor found that this increased self esteem "was often manifested in producers' behavior relative to others in their community, such as increased participation in public assemblies." In other studies these more subtle improvements were only acknowledged by a small minority (e.g. of only 14 % in a case study in El Salvador).

Other indirect benefits of participation in Fair Trade reported in case studies are increased spending on education of children. and the preservation of indigenous cultures. It must however be noted that the evidence for the claim that high proportions of the extra income through Fair Trade is spent on education and that Fair Trade supports the survival of indigenous cultures is more anecdotal than systematic and that other factors like low success rates in schools or powerful trends like urbanization and migration may neutralize these impacts.

An important issue in Fair Trade is the apparent gender bias. A variety of studies has shown, that since the income generated from Fair Trade crops is generally controlled by male household members, and since less woman are employed in Fair Trade cooperatives, there is no or little female empowerment or improvement of the livelihoods of woman through Fair Trade. Sometimes more women are employed but men still get the income. Often specific woman empowerment programs are required by the certifiers but the implementation seems hard. And as Mayoux has pointed out, if females are employed in Fair Trade their workload often increases since they are not exempt from household work. There are however also positive examples: In a producer organization in India in the increased participation of females in the production process had broader impacts like "increase in self-confidence, economic independence, better access to health, and participation in decision-making in the family, community, and local council."

[...]

Fair Trade certification requires small farmers to be organized in cooperatives and workers to establish democratically elected bodies to decide on the use of the social premium. It is important to note the mutually supportive effects of Fair Trade and cooperatives. Cooperatives enhance producer power in local markets, increase income for both members and non-members by creating competition to private intermediaries and democratically empower its members to express their voices collectively. Milford has shown in a study on cooperatives in Chiapas, Mexico, that cooperatives often failed if they were not involved in selling for the Fair Trade market. If cooperatives are engaged in Fair Trade, they cannot only compete better in the conventional market but Fair Trade also works better in generating cooperative and organizational benefits then other financial and developmental support by NGOs or governments. Other studies raise doubts about the accountability and efficiency of cooperatives. A study from a coffee cooperative in Nicaragua argues that the cooperative as a organizational structure "involves an expensive, top-heavy entrepreneurial hierarchy, including a large administrative staff and substantial representation costs for its leaders." Several studies revealed a lack of "effective democracy" in large cooperatives and even the emergence of a new "management class" (and there have even been reports of corruption.

Other organizational benefits that have been highlighted in several studies are access to market information and the increased credibility of producer organizations that participate in Fair Trade. All these aspects have helped many producer cooperatives their performance in the non-Fair Trade market, often enabling small farmer coffee organizations to establish direct links with foreign companies, sometimes under conditions similar to Fair Trade. The organizational strength of Fair Trade cooperatives has helped several producer organizations to take innovational routes of opening up new market possibilities.

[...]

Efficacy of Fair Trade

There is still a lack of consistent research on the impact and the effectiveness of Fair Trade. Especially the attempts to come up with quantifiable methods of calculating if the money spent on Fair Trade products or donated to Fair Trade organizations is well spent, is only in its preliminary stages. Since all the impact studies conclude that the most important benefits of Fair Trade are non-monetary, quantitative assessments can only capture one part of the entire impact that Fair Trade has on producers. The non-monetary impact on the life of producers is hard to quantify, but the qualitative research summarized above should give some insight. Nicholls & Opal attempted to use a quantitative and highly sophisticated account to measure the social return on investment for a South African wine cooperative and found with this somewhat contingent and problematic method that "for every £1 spent on Fair Trade wine (at the import level), a value of £6.89 was returned to the community."

Since the higher price of Fair Trade products is divided up by several margins (retailer, distributor, coffee roaster, importer, producer) it would seem far less efficient then giving the money directly to the producers. There has not been a systematic account yet. While some studies suggest that a reasonable percentage of the extra price for Fair Trade actually reaches producers, other reports seem to imply that sometimes Fair Trade is a pretty inefficient way to transfer money to producers in the South. In a critical article in the *Wall Street Journal* Stecklow & White have reported some examples that show how Northern retailers benefit far more than the producers from Fair Trade: At Sainsbury's, a British supermarket chain, the price of Fair Trade bananas (which was four times that of conventional bananas) was US$2.74 per pound. The producers receive only 16 cents per pound, 55 cent go to all the middlemen and importers and the rest to the supermarket, which earns approximately US$2 with every pound of organic Fair Trade bananas.[5] At a *Cafe Borders* in New York City, producers paid nearly US$12 a pound for bags of Fair Trade coffee while farmers received only US$1.41. A comparative study of the coffee supply chain of *Nestlé* and the Fair Trade supplier *Cafédirect* found that out of the 34 percent Fair Trade mark-up for the consumer price only 4 percent ended up with the producers, mainly due to higher costs of advertisement and marketing licence. Zehner compared Fair Trade coffee and conventional coffee and found that 43 percent of the higher price of US$1.50 is passed on to producers while

39 percent went into the increased margin of Starbucks itself. And there are more similar examples.

This is however not the general rule. Other retailers, by selling Fair Trade products at the same price as conventional products, have shown the way to increase the market share of Fair Trade and to decrease exclusion on the side of consumers. At the supermarket chain *Migros* in Switzerland for example Fair Trade bananas have almost the same price as non-Fair Trade bananas (which made it possible to increase the market share of Fair Trade banana to 56 percent) and *Wild Oats Natural Marketplace* in the U.S. sells Fair Trade bananas and bulk coffee at the same price as their conventional counterparts. To change this situation, in which consumers pay very high prices with the intention of helping producers, but end up mostly increasing the margin of the retailer, it would be interesting to investigate the possibility of establishing a further criterion for Fair Trade certification, ruling that the margins of retailers cannot be higher for Fair Trade products than for conventional products. A related criterion could be to make all retailers of Fair Trade products disclose their margins, something many retailers refuse to do.[6] Another problem is the inefficiency of many Fair Trade supply chains. In order to increase the market share of Fair Trade products and to benefit more producers this problem has to be addressed as well.

[…]

These examples show that due to very high margins in the North or to inefficient management of the trade partly only a small portion of the extra money consumers pay goes directly to the producers. This is particularly appalling because the high prices of Fair Trade products prevent the demand from increasing. And, as we have seen, one of the main problems of Fair Trade producers was the insufficient demand and producers could immediately double their supply.

[…]

Notes

1. For a further discussion of these difficulties see Mayoux (2001) and Nicholls & Opal (2005: 201).

2. A report of the Fair Trade coffee market in Latin America that is based on seven case studies concludes, for example, by exclusively citing the most positive study (Perezgrovas and Cervantes, 2002), concluding (and thereby implying this as the general finding) that the direct financial "revenues for Fair Trade coffee [are] twice the street price for conventional coffee, even after deductions were made for cooperative management and other expenses." (Murray et al, 2003: 7). Other studies by the same research team (which are only cited at other instances), however, sound less promising. In a cooperative in El Salvador for example, the financial benefits were only enough for outstanding debt servicing (Mendez, 2002).

3. But to put this into perspective it is interesting to note that more or less the same amount (€ 18.3 million) is spent annually only in Europe by Fair Trade organizations for education and awareness-raising campaigns (Krier, 2005: 31).

4. And even most studies point at several advantages of Fair Trade. Robbert Maseland and Albert de Vaal (2002) at the University of Nijmegen in Holland for example compared Fair Trade with free trade and protectionism and concluded that it was "obvious" that Fair Trade is the only way to guarantee the fulfilment of minimum requirements such as stopping child labour or environmentally harmful effects. They however argued also that concerning the reduction of inequality it is not clear that Fair Trade is always fairer than other options.

5. "Sainsbury's, which says it sells more fair-trade bananas than any other British supermarket, sells the fruit in bagged bunches of six, not by weight. A bag of fair-trade Dominican Republic bananas, weighing about a pound, recently cost around $2.74 in London. That's more than four times the price of a pound of unbagged regular bananas, also from the Dominican Republic. According to FLO, Dominican Republic fair-trade banana growers receive about 16 cents a pound from middlemen. Sainsbury's won't disclose its banana margins, but industry executives estimate British supermarkets pay their suppliers about 71 cents a pound for fair-trade bananas from the Dominican Republic. If that's the case, Sainsbury's is earning almost $2 a pound."

6. This claim totally goes against what Paul Rice, chief executive of Transfair USA argues: "As a core philosophy, Fair Traders believe in as little market intervention as possible [and: regulating retail prices goes against the idea of] using the market as a vehicle for creating a win-win scenario for farmers and for industry." The growth of fair-trade sales in the U.S. suggests "millions of U.S. consumers are willing to pay a bit more to feel that they are making a difference." (Stecklow & White, 2004)

Fair Trade Improves the Lives of the Impoverished

Elen Jones

Elen Jones is the national coordinator for Fair Trade Wales.

When I visited the Mbale region of eastern Uganda, I wasn't sure what I was going to see. I had heard that Fairtrade provides education, access to health, better terms of trade, minimum prices, respect for the environment and perhaps most importantly, connection with the consumer and hope for the future. But is it true? Could something so vital in a capitalist world, really deliver all of this?

As I made my way from the capital, Kampala, on the 5 hour journey on one of the worst roads I had ever been on, passing through slums and landfill sites littered with people trying to carve out an existence, I left the haze of browns and greys, the hustle and bustle of busy city life and entered miles upon miles of green, luscious sugar and tea plantations. A reminder of the concept that thousands of miles away, poor people are working hard to provide us with the things we need.

As I reached the town of Mbale, a busy and active typical African looking town, I was keen to visit Mwenyi Rd; home to the Gumutindo Coffee Co-operative factory that I had heard so much about before my trip. It has been certified by Fairtrade International since 2004, and appears to have grown from strength to strength.

Access to Work, Childcare, and Minimum Pay

I was keen to meet the workers, to find out for myself what life was really like. Most of them are women. Some are from the Namatala slums, where the factory provides free childcare, free lunch and a

"Why I'm Certain Fairtrade Delivers Benefits to Farmers," by Elen Jones, Fair Trade Wales. Reprinted by permission.

minimum wage in exchange for their immense skills in selecting only the best high quality coffee beans for the global market. One woman told me that *"there is nowhere as good as here. I have good pay, food and know my children are safe. I like being with the other women too."*

Co-Operative Impact

From here, I headed east, into the Budduda district, an area prone to mudslides. A landscape that reminded me of home, Wales. Sadly, thousands of people have been injured or buried alive in recent years, due to climate change bringing unpredictable heavier rains, which are hard to respond to quickly enough. Here I visited the coffee store and met hundreds of farmers, who told me that if it had not been for Fairtrade, they would not be able to survive. The price they get for their coffee is higher than ever before, and more than they could have imagined. They no longer have to climb Mount Elgon, across to Kenya, to sell their coffee on the open market to get what they can. They are part of a co-operative; a primary society among 9 others that sell to Gumutindo Coffee Co-operative. They get the best price, as their coffee is organic and they benefit from the guaranteed minimum price set by Fairtrade International. The 5% premium that they get on top is spent on projects decided by the primary society board members, who are elected democratically and must have women representatives. I was surprised to see more women than men on some of the societies.

Education and Climate Change

I asked to see where the premium had been spent. I was keen to see with my own eyes, the impacts and the difference Fairtrade reported to provide. I was blown away. Not only were the societies deciding for themselves, but they had vision and hope that took my breath away. They had action plans on coloured card on walls of the schools and the offices. The community was working as whole, to ensure that the farmers' success was having the greatest impact possible. I saw classrooms, solar panels, cow sharing schemes, water provision and water storage, and the planting of trees. I witnessed one of the 1st tree saplings being planted as part of the Size of Wales, million-tree scheme, a partnership response to climate change. I met people who had suffered from malaria, and thanks to the community Fairtrade premium, had been given medication. The children who had been left orphans because of HIV/Aids went to school, had uniforms and food. All paid for from the Fairtrade premium.

There is no doubt in my mind, that when I see the FAIRTRADE logo back here in the UK, that I know it does what it says and that there is no other label or certification process that can guarantee all of this. It may have a long way to go; and it was never a one-size fits all or fix-all, but empowering farmers to take hold of their own destiny and develop their own community sustainably is a truly wonderful outcome.

Irresponsible and Inaccurate Reporting

I have seen and witnessed the benefits of Fairtrade in action and the dramatic improvements made to people's lives first hand. So when I see what appears to be erroneous, sensationalist news headlines and read a research report that appears to not only give inaccurate information, but also uses unbalanced research methods that discredits what I know to be true, I become sad and angry. I expect better from the UK press than to publish potentially distorted and prejudiced articles garnered from lazy reporting and fact checking. I expect a balanced open debate. It appears that the research project not only failed to compare like-for-like e.g fairtrade smallholder farm versus non-fairtrade large-scale farms, but it also appears that some facts included and used to justify its findings, are inaccurate.

We welcome research, it is important; it helps us be better. It allows us to recognise success, highlight issues, investigate them further and make necessary improvements. However, is it responsible to give such exposure to research that appears neither balanced or accurate? I worry for those farmers that truly benefit from Fairtrade, and the impact this kind of publication can have on them. I wish that unfettered capitalism received the same level of scrutiny that trade justice appears to receive. I will certainly not allow one research paper to undermine my own opinion of a truly amazing model of trade and international sustainable development, that of course has its faults and is still in its adolescence, but despite that, delivers some truly wonderful and vital outcomes.

I agree with Mike Gidney, Chief Executive of the Fairtrade Foundation in that *"it is wrong to say that Fairtrade does not improve the lives of the poor."* I've seen it with my own eyes. Since 2005 we have had more than 50 Fairtrade farmer visits to Wales, all of whom have told their story and the positive impact Fairtrade has had on their lives and their communities. Were they all wrong too?

How Fair Trade Maintains Poverty

Andrew Chambers

Andrew Chambers is a journalist at the Guardian *with a focus in international development. He is also a teacher in Thailand.*

Nestlé has just announced that KitKat—Britain's biggest-selling chocolate bar—will carry the Fairtrade logo from next month. But how much do consumers really know about the Fairtrade movement? Is it, as some say, an essential safety net that helps poor farmers earn a better living or, as others say, an example of western feel-good tokenism that holds back modernisation and entrenches agrarian poverty?

There are now more than 4,500 Fairtrade items on our shelves. UK sales boomed by 43% in 2008 and the British government has announced a four-year £15m funding package for the organisation.

Fairtrade provides a minimum baseline price for commodities, allowing farmers to hedge against market volatility. The co-operative system allows small farmers better access to global markets and encourages democratic representation. Each commodity price also includes a "social premium" which can be reinvested in social or development projects.

However, economist Paul Collier argues that Fairtrade effectively ensures that people "get charity as long as they stay producing the crops that have locked them into poverty." Fairtrade reduces the incentive to diversify crop production and encourages the utilisation of resources on marginal land that could be better employed for other produce. The organisation also appears wedded to an image of a notional anti-modernist rural idyll. Farm units must remain small and family run, while modern farming techniques (mechanisation, economies of scale, pesticides, genetic modification etc) are sidelined or even actively discouraged.

Fairtrade director of communications Barbara Cowther admitted in the documentary A Bitter Aftertaste that the organisation had no real policy on mechanisation—this despite the fact that it is central to agricultural development.

By guaranteeing a minimum price, Fairtrade also encourages market oversupply, which depresses global commodity prices. This locks Fairtrade farmers into greater Fairtrade dependency and further impoverishes farmers outside the Fairtrade umbrella. Economist Tyler Cowen describes this as the "parallel exploitation coffee sector."

Coffee farms must not be more than 12 acres in size and they are not allowed to employ any full-time workers. This means that during harvest season migrant workers must be employed on short-term contracts. These rural poor are therefore expressly excluded from the stability of long-term employment by Fairtrade rules. Indeed, The International Development Committee declared in 2007 that "Fairtrade could have a deeper impact if it were to target more consciously the poorest of the poor."

We might think of sub-Saharan subsistence economies when we think of Fairtrade, but the biggest recipient of Fairtrade subsidy is actually Mexico. Mexico is the biggest producer of Fairtrade coffee with about 23% market share. Indeed, as of 2002, 181 of the 300 Fairtrade coffee producers were located in South America and the Caribbean. As Marc Sidwell points out, while Mexico has 51 Fairtrade producers, Burundi has none, Ethiopia four and Rwanda just 10—meaning that "Fairtrade pays to support relatively wealthy Mexican coffee farmers at the expense of poorer nations."

Another criticism is over institutional inefficiencies. The vast majority of the money from Fairtrade sales remains in the west—with only about 5% of the Fairtrade sale price actually making it back to the farmers. As Philip Oppenheim says, "any intelligent person will ask why I should pay 80p more for my bananas when only 5p will end up with the producer." Fundamental to the failure of wealth transfer are issues such as the fact that while 90% of the world's cocoa is produced in the developing world, only 4% of the chocolate is produced there. Developing countries remain locked in the primary sector commodities market, while the west cashes in on their value-added conversion.

Colleen Berndt of George Mason University details how Fairtrade membership can also be high. The costs take in not just certification and annual inspections, but also the wider compliance with Fairtrade organisational structures. In Guatemala, an executive at Fedecocagua, the country's biggest Fairtrade co-operative, admitted that "after paying for the co-operative's employees and programmes, nothing remained of the Fairtrade premiums to be passed on to the individual farmers."

A further inefficiency is highlighted by examining the accounts of the independent charity Fairtrade Foundation, which licenses the use of the Fairtrade mark in the UK. In 2008, of a total income of £7.2m, the largest expenditure was on "public education and awareness" at more than £2.1m. Fairtrade is an expensive brand to maintain because it relies solely on consumer awareness campaigns, and these costs eat into the Fairtrade premiums that farmers can receive.

Ultimately, Daniel Jaffee concludes that "Fairtrade ... does not bring the majority of participants out of poverty." He suggests the small increase in farmers' wages is at the expense of further entrenching the agrarian status quo, disadvantaging migrant workers and those outside the Fairtrade organisation. Steve Daily, of WorldWrite charity, condemns the movement for having horizons that are far too low, and for not focusing enough on actual agricultural reform. Berndt concludes that Fairtrade coffee can provide a useful short-term hedge against commodity volatility, but that in the long run it "represents at best a Band-Aid to the problems that coffee producing nations face."

The Fairtrade concept itself still has merit—and as long as protectionist trade barriers limit commodities entering western markets there will be a place for developing world trade subsidies.

However, a greater focus on producing and exporting western consumables would ensure that much more of the Fairtrade price went back to the developing world. Larger land units and greater mechanisation could help drive agricultural development. An increase in the commodity social tariff would help social progress. Fairtrade could also allow western consumers to donate directly to this social fund—providing a more efficient mechanism for charitable transfer than currently exists. It is not time to ditch Fairtrade, but it is time that there was an intelligent debate about how the organisation can employ its massive consumer goodwill to best help lift agrarian workers out of poverty.

Free Trade, Not Fair Trade

Gene Callahan

Gene Callahan is a professor of economics at the State University of New York at Purchase and the author of Economics for Real People.

We've all seen the signs in our local cafes, boasting something like: "We proudly sell coffee brewed with Fair Trade coffee beans, acquired at a price that permits sustainable farming and pays growers a living wage." These posters are part of a popular trend in "progressive" circles to promote "fair trade." For some reason, perhaps because many of these folks get really hyped up on Joe every day, fair trade in coffee seems to be the chief focus of the movement.

According to the latest data I could turn up on the Internet, fair-trade coffee buyers must pay at least $1.50 per pound if the spot price on the commodities market is lower than that figure. If the market price is higher, they will pay a 5-cent-per-pound premium over the going rate. (The exact current numbers, if they have changed, are unimportant to our analysis.) I'm not clear how the "fair" price was determined to be $1.50, rather than $1.46 or $1.59 or even $20.00, but so be it. The fair traders evidently believe that growers who cannot make a profit at the market price ought to be helped to stay in business anyway. (To what extent the current market price is a free-market price will be examined shortly.) They find it unfair that, in the words of the website Global Exchange: "Many small coffee farmers receive prices for their coffee that are less than the costs of production, forcing them into a cycle of poverty and debt."

There are two possible causes of the situation described by Global Exchange. In some cases it may be that a particular farmer could run his business profitably except that he is competing

"Is Fair Trade a Fair Deal?" by Gene Callahan, Foundation for Economic Education, March 1, 2008. https://fee.org/articles/is-fair-trade-a-fair-deal/. Licensed under CC BY 4.0 International.

against others who receive some form of state-granted privilege, for instance, a direct subsidy from their own government or favorable terms of trade from some coffee-importing country. That is clearly unjust, but I contend that the best way to address such injustice is to eliminate the favoritism, rather than trying to compensate for it.

On the other hand, considering that the phenomenon of unprofitable coffee farmers is widespread, it also appears likely that there are simply too many producers in the world relative to the demand for their output. (And, of course, for any particular instance of a money-losing plantation, both factors may be relevant: the farm in question might do better than it does at present if it faced no subsidized competitors, while still falling short of profitability.) To whatever extent the second cause is to blame for the plight of growers, the only long-term, effective remedy is that a sufficient number of those farming at a loss exit the industry so as to permit the remaining producers to operate at a profit. (I am using "profit" here in the accounting sense, meaning an excess of income over expenses, and not in the economic sense of an above-normal return on capital.)

Advising struggling Third World coffee farmers simply to abandon their trade and find another way to make a living may seem flippant and heartless, especially coming from a well-off First World resident who is not confronted with such a daunting prospect. But I suggest that the compassionate concern apparently motivating that initial reaction is only superficial since it ignores two hard realities. First, continuing to operate a money-losing business in the absence of a scheme that plausibly could reverse its fortunes merely makes one's financial predicament more and more dire. If the situation does not appear likely to change for the foreseeable future, then even relaxing in a hammock all day is a better business plan than continuing to grow coffee at a loss. The former option at least stops the bleeding.

Second, it is ludicrous to imagine that a social arrangement is sustainable in which anyone who chooses to persist in a money-losing occupation is entitled to be supported in his obstinacy by the rest of his society. If all members of a society decided to follow their own inner calling without regard to the needs and desires of their fellows, soon enough there would be no resources available to support the pursuit of their visions. A prosperous society can afford to maintain a certain number of commercially disdainful artists, mendicant religious ascetics, selfless social reformers, unworldly scholars, and carefree "dharma bums," but only through the efforts of the bulk of its members who grow food, build houses, produce clothing, treat diseases, collect garbage, discourage criminality and violence, and perform all of the other jobs meeting the more mundane requirements of orderly social existence.

Since the very possibility of following a way of life indifferent to material concerns depends on the output of a multitude of others who are attending to those matters, people choosing the former course have no right to demand as their due any share of the resources produced by those opting for the latter course; rather, the visionaries' just claim for support could lie only in persuading their more-worldly companions voluntarily to aid them in their mission. It is the responsibility of every minimally functional adult to discover how she can perform some activity that others value enough to provide her with her sustenance, whether those others express that valuation by commercial transactions or ideal-inspired donations.

In light of the inescapable requirement that, for a society to continue, its members on net must engage in genuinely productive—meaning remunerative—activities, I can conceive of no plausible case for singling out coffee farmers as members of a special class that is exempt from pulling at least its own weight.

If we reject on principle the notion that any interest group has a rightful claim to such a privileged economic status, it does not imply that we lack sympathy for the real hardships likely to face a poor, largely uneducated peasant whose whole working life has been spent farming coffee and who must abandon the one occupation he knows well for the uncertain promise that he can do better elsewhere. But I suggest that those seeking to ameliorate that peasant's plight are well advised to direct whatever funds and energy they would devote to that aim toward helping him learn a new, more viable trade rather than using them to postpone the day when he must face up to his real situation.

Somewhat ironically, if fair traders choose to follow the second alternative, it is likely they will wind up even further depressing the coffee price confronting any farmers who are not producing fair-trade beans, since each consumer who switches to the fair-trade product is one less buyer for the "un-fair" coffee traded on the commodity market. "But," fair traders may protest, "our ultimate goal is that all coffee purchased be fair-trade coffee, so that all growers will receive the higher, fair-trade price!" However, even if that seemingly implausible scenario comes to be realized, the fair-trade movement still could not succeed in securing for every current coffee farmer a higher income than he receives today. A fundamental principle of economics is that the quantity of a good demanded drops when its price increases, meaning that at the universally higher price for coffee the fair-trade campaign would achieve by reaching its final aim, consumers would drink less of the beverage and the current glut of coffee farmers only would be exacerbated.

I suggest that this belief in the power of some concerned body—be it composed of government officials, economic "experts," religious authorities, or social activists—to discern some "just price" for a good, other than the one emerging from the market process, is the most fundamental misunderstanding bedeviling the fair-trade movement.

Arbitrary-Selection

However, that is not the only problem with its present modus operandi. At least in its current corporate embodiment in the company bearing the name TransFair USA, which is the entity that officially labels certain coffees "Fair Trade," the movement appears somewhat arbitrary about which producers are to be blessed with the label. Kerry Howley, writing in the March

2006 *Reason* magazine, describes the predicament of farmers like Gregorio Martinez, who owns a small, family-operated plantation in Honduras. In the course of operating his business he overcame severe hardships, including the destruction of an entire year's crop by Hurricane Mitch and the threat of imminent foreclosure, to eventually win an important international prize for his product. It might seem that Martinez is just the kind of farmer the fair-trade movement ought to be promoting, but TransFair USA will only certify growers who are part of a cooperative, and so he cannot sell his beans with the "Fair Trade" label. Similarly, in Africa, many coffee farms are deemed ineligible for the label because they are run in a more traditional tribal style rather than in the democratic fashion demanded by the Eurocentric arbiters of who deserves the "Fair Trade" imprimatur.

Marching under the fair-trade banner along with such dubious company are some genuinely promising initiatives. For instance, the effort to convince consumers to purchase "shade-grown" coffee instead of coffee produced in the monocultural method more common today, in which the crop is grown in a cleared field, is a plausible way to help maintain biodiversity. The natural setting of the coffee plant is as an understory shrub in dense forests, meaning that farmers can grow it under a canopy of trees, which may yield profitable crops themselves. Growing coffee under shade certainly results in a more natural environment than having large swathes of land occupied by only one plant species; it's an environment much friendlier to animal life and perhaps even helpful in slowing global warming. And consumers who buy shade-grown coffee at a higher price than that of coffee grown on a monocultural plantation are not attempting to supplant the market process with their own, arbitrary judgments about what various goods "ought" to cost, but are acting through that process to express their preference for a healthier, more vital environment. Indeed, to an extent that could only be determined by a detailed historical study quite beyond the scope and aim of this article, it was not the market that chose the current predominance of high-tech, monocultural coffee production, but governmental policies. As Deborah James of the Center for Economic and Policy Research notes, "In the 1970s the United States Agency for International Development (USAID) gave over $80 million to coffee plantations in Latin America to 'modernize'—to strip coffee of shade trees and purchase chemical pesticides and fertilizers."

"Bird-friendly" coffee, as far as I can determine by my (admittedly limited) reading on the subject, is just an alternate name for "shade-grown" coffee—the trees above the coffee plants provide homes and resting places for birds—so buying it is similarly defensible. And if organic farming is really preferable to "chemical farming"—which is a disputed contention, since it is unclear where all the inputs needed for productive organic farming, such as manure, would come from if everyone forswore industrially manufactured fertilizers and pesticides—then buying organic coffee may also make sense.

Another plank of the fair-trade platform, advocating that consumers purchase coffee only from producers who embrace a minimum standard of decent working conditions for the agricultural laborers growing and harvesting their beans, cannot be ruled out on its face as a possible means of improving the lot of those impoverished workers. If some relatively wealthy residents of developed countries are willing to pay a higher coffee price to benefit poor farm hands, their intention is entirely laudable. However, I think the right approach here is to shop for a guarantee of labor standards while letting the market determine what the price for those standards will be, not to attempt to guess at a "just" price and pray that it makes everything all right.

Furthermore, anyone deciding to pursue this course should remain keenly aware there is no "silver bullet" with which to slay the beast named Third World Poverty. Even given that consumers are willing to pay a higher price for coffee produced under stricter labor standards, that labor will still be more costly to the farm owner, meaning that, at the margin, he will find it profitable to use more capital, such as machines or fertilizer, and less labor than he would under less-stringent labor requirements. It is inevitable that fewer workers will be employed under the improved conditions than would have been in their absence. The net result still may be preferable to the situation that existed before the consumers' campaign for higher labor standards. But if activists are really concerned about the well-being of the people they purport to be helping, and not just their own satisfaction in having adopted a noble cause, then their judgment of whether a real improvement is likely to occur ought to be based on both the positive and negative effects of their actions and not on a naïve faith that good intentions necessarily yield good outcomes.

The fair traders' broad criticisms of the current institutional foundation on which the global coffee industry is built also are justified, at least for those who advocate a free society, since the current world coffee market could hardly be termed "free." The coffee market itself is directly subject to many politically motivated distortions. For example, Kendra Okonski of the London-based International Policy Network points to recent policies adopted by the government of Vietnam as contributing significantly to the "coffee crisis." State officials, encouraged by international agencies to undertake "market reforms," decided to turn the country into a major coffee exporter, with the result that the nation, as of 2006, was the world's second-largest producer. The government subsidized producers, assisted in its project by low-cost loans to Vietnamese coffee farmers made by French, German, and Swiss government aid agencies, at a time when coffee prices were high.

But only looking at direct state interventions in the coffee market would seriously underestimate the full impact of state policies on the industry. As Okonski notes, an even "bigger problem is highly subsidized farmers in wealthy countries. Huge subsidies to farmers in parts of the West mean that farmers in poor countries cannot diversify their production, because they cannot access these markets. Poor farmers choose to produce coffee, cocoa and other commodities because they have few other options with which to generate income." Furthermore, developed countries put high tariffs and import quotas on processed agricultural goods, discouraging the development of valued-added processing industries in the Third World.

Land Theft

The final major deviation of the contemporary coffee market from a genuinely free market that I will note is that the existing pattern of land holdings, in all countries but especially in many of the Third World nations that produce the crop, is hardly the outcome of purely voluntary exchanges. Rather, it owes much of its current shape to past acts of theft, fraud, and highly coercive or manipulated transactions masquerading as trades on a free market. Indigenous people robbed of the land that supported them, land with which their intimate familiarity may have been their most valuable social capital, often were left with no better option than to toil at the behest of their expropriators on whatever miserable terms they were offered, and the lamentable effects of such injustices are still with us today.

As a result of such recent government interventions and past exploitations, farmers who are not the beneficiaries of policy favoritism may find themselves operating at a great disadvantage compared to those who are luckier in that respect. That situation is certainly deplorable. But I can't see that consumer action would be a promising way to rectify those inequities. How can a coffee shopper be expected to keep track of just which producers are getting just what advantages due to government policies and correctly calculate just what price he should pay to offset the effects of those state-granted privileges? No, it seems to me that the only sensible approach is to fight against the unfair policies directly, at the ballot box, through op-eds, by lobbying, and so on. Perhaps individual buying decisions can have some impact in the meantime, but their effect is likely to be minuscule compared to the scope of the problems.

In short, I see the Fair Trade movement as embodying a mixture of sound ideas for improving the state of the coffee industry and well-meaning but misguided attempts to fight the realities of supply and demand. The latter stem, I believe, from the misconception, common in Progressive circles, that the free market is a merely contingent feature of human social life, rigged up by the powerful to enable their exploitation of the weak. To the contrary, as brilliantly demonstrated by Ludwig von Mises and F. A. Hayek, the market process is the only method for rationally allocating scarce resources in any advanced economy. The mistaken view of many Progressives stems, to some extent, from a simple lack of economic understanding. But their mistrust of free markets also is bolstered by the fact that apologists for the many current situations in which the powerful have manipulated government rules and policies to entrench and increase their privileged positions in society often attempt to disguise the true character of what is going on by claiming that those outcomes are the result of free-market decisions, and, as such, perfectly just. Therefore, it is vital that advocates of truly free markets work to expose such deceit for what it is.

A genuinely free market favors no one except those who best can produce the goods desired by consumers, and no participant in the market process can gain an elevated status in society that is exempt from the necessity to continue to serve the interests of consumers in the future. If Progressives, who typically are driven by a truly commendable desire for a fair society, come to recognize that moving toward genuinely free markets will advance, and not hinder, the achievement of their goals, then their efforts will achieve much better results, to the benefit of everyone except the entrenched interests that profit from the current, government-distorted markets.

Fair Trade Is Incompatible with the Rules of Economics and Fails Producers

Ndongo Samba Sylla

Ndongo Samba Sylla is a Senegalese development economist. He is also the author of the Fair Trade Scandal: Marketing Poverty to Benefit the Rich.

In response to the growing demand of citizens in developed countries for quality consumption, the proliferation of "ethical labels" is simply staggering. For some, the purchase and consumption of goods has become a political act. News that Green & Black's new chocolate bar will be neither organic nor Fairtrade-certified—instead, the beans have been sourced via certified scheme Cocoa Life—has caused controversy, while the world's biggest Fairtrade retailer, Sainsbury's, recently came under fire for dropping the Fairtrade label from its own-brand tea.

Most of these so-called ethical retailers and schemes—Cocoa Life included—are certainly, to my mind, not driven by "ethics." Fairtrade, at least, was a grassroots movement aiming for changes from below, which is not always the case for the ethical labels used by some supermarkets and retailers. Those who introduce ethical labels just want to position themselves in a growing market and make a profit—and under these conditions, it is not easy for the average consumer to distinguish tares from wheat.

The Fairtrade (FT) mark is one of the most well-known and respected labels in the world, with an economic model that aims to improve the living conditions of rural producers of the global south in a solidarity approach with consumers in the north. The objective is to facilitate access to the markets of the north, to guarantee them decent prices and to eliminate the "unfair" middlemen exploiting them.

"Fairtrade Only Really Benefits Supermarkets. A Rethink Is Needed," by Ndongo Samba Sylla, Guardian News and Media Limited, August 4, 2017. Reprinted by permission.

Unfortunately, the FT economic model has significant limitations that continue to generate legitimate criticism.

The FT movement is regularly accused of working with companies that have behaved unethically in the past or that are considered symbols of the unfairness of the international trading system. What is often highlighted is the gulf between the principles of the FT movement and its practices. This moral criticism, however, is insufficient. Economic criticism from the perspective of producers is needed as well.

The FT economic model faces a structural contradiction. On the one hand, if the minimum price for FT products is high, they may not find outlets. Sales will be low. The economic benefits to producer organisations will also be negligible. On the other hand, if the minimum price of FT products is "competitive," sales may increase but the impact in terms of poverty reduction will be insignificant. Besides, due to the fierce competition caused by the proliferation of labels, the FT movement is induced to "lower" its standards—conservative minimum prices, lower requirements in terms of FT content for composite products, etc—in the hope of boosting its sales. So, it should not be a surprise that in some contexts, non-FT producers are better off than comparable FT producers. This kind of hard evidence is often downplayed by the FT movement.

Faced with the contradiction between the marketing logic of sales growth and the logic of poverty reduction at a very small scale, the FT movement has until now privileged the former.

Fairtrade protagonists tend to assert that the FT model is an alternative to the "free market"—but the reality is that it is a "parenthesis" within the conventional trading system. Once the rules of the game are laid down (financing, minimum prices, premiums, traceability), market access and prices are determined on a competitive basis, as in the case of conventional trade.

FT labelling organisations cannot guarantee that buyers involved in the movement will pay producers' organisations a price higher than the FT minimum price. Nor can they guarantee that producer organisations can sell all their FT-certified production under FT conditions (payment of minimum prices and premiums). According to figures provided by Fairtrade International for 2013-2014, only 28% of FT coffee was sold in FT markets. Fairtrade bananas are the bestselling product (56%-64%), while FT tea is the least sold product (7%). In other words, supply is higher than demand for all FT products.

Owing to free market principles, producer organisations that usually join the FT movement are not necessarily the poorest, but those that can meet market demands—ie those with the means to afford certification fees and a certain scale of production. No wonder producer organisations from the least developed countries tend to be under-represented.

A further issue regarding the FT model is the maintaining of countries of the south in a disadvantageous economic specialisation. While most of them have been exporting primary commodities since colonial times, this has not led to economic transformations beneficial to the vast majority of their populations.

The FT movement as a whole would have more impact if it focused on manufactured goods produced using local agricultural products. This type of model would have the advantage of generating productive employment and stimulating technological innovation in the countries of the south.

Recent Studies of Fair Trade Show That Producers Still Face Financial Instability

Sanjay Lanka and Steffen Böhm

Sanjay Lanka is a PhD candidate at the University of Essex in the United Kingdom focusing on sustainability accounting. Steffen Böhm is a professor of organization and sustainability at the University of Essex.

Two weeks of campaigning to raise awareness of Fairtrade products have come to a close. But coffee farmers around the world face an ongoing crisis that the Fairtrade Foundation has done little to mitigate and more must be done to address the problems they face of plummeting prices.

Fairtrade is based on a vision to provide marginal farmers with a sustainable livelihood. Yet, farmers are not protected by Fairtrade in the current coffee price crisis and they are struggling to meet the basic costs of production, never mind make a living.

Financial (In)stability

Fairtrade started as an effort to mitigate the crises caused by crashes in commodity prices, such as coffee, helping farmers in the developing world to live a decent life. The Fairtrade Foundation claims that it covers the average costs of production, thereby ensuring a sustainable livelihood for the farmers and their families. It hopes to provide a degree of financial stability to the farmers through long-term trading relationships that provide access to pre-finance access to credit, enabling the farmers to plan their production and invest in the necessary agricultural inputs.

Our fieldwork, undertaken in Costa Rica, Nicaragua and India since 2009, tells a different story. In these countries, some farmers

"Fair for Who? The Crisis of Fairtrade for Coffee Farmers," by Sanjay Lanka and Steffen Böhm, The Conversation, March 13, 2014. https://theconversation.com/fair-for-who-the-crisis-of-fairtrade-for-coffee-farmers-24254. Licensed under CC BY 4.0 International.

are leaving the Fairtrade scheme since it does not always cover the basic costs of production.

To redress this criticism, in 2011 Fairtrade increased its floor price from US$2.64/kg to US$3.08/kg and also doubled the Fairtrade premium to US$0.44/kg of coffee added to the price. This must be seen in the context of the fall in coffee price on the international market from around US$6.77/kg in 2011 to US$2.55/kg at the end of 2013.

Fairtrade "producer prices" are prices paid to a co-operative of farmers. To be viable for the farmers, they should cover not only the costs of production of the individual farmers, but also the cost of operating the Fairtrade co-operative. This also relates to the processing of coffee beans to enable their export to Fairtrade markets.

Making Ends Meet

These costs do not decrease when the international market price of coffee drops. In one of the co-operatives that we studied, their cost of production in 2012-13 was US$6.54/kg plus an overhead cost of US$3.27/kg for export-ready coffee while the price on the international market for this was only US$2.13/kg. Hence, there is a limited relationship between the actual costs and the market price.

Even with the Fairtrade floor price and premium, the price would usually be no more than about $3.50/kg which would still not cover the costs of production. This premium must be invested by the co-operative in various projects to improve the lives of its members and their communities, which is a good thing. But, since most of this money is spent at the community level, it does not provide enough income to individual farmers.

To supplement this, co-operatives might join a plethora of other organisations with their own requirements for accountability. All of these different systems with their additional costs must then be maintained by the co-operative.

Diversification and Uniformity

Despite a variation among coffee growing countries in terms of their labour, input and living costs, the Fairtrade floor price and premium are the same worldwide as determined by the Fairtrade Foundation. This ensures that the Fairtrade retail partners have a guaranteed price irrespective of the coffee's origin. This emphasis of the Fairtrade market on export seems to perpetuate a dependency relationship with Northern buyers.

Co-operatives that have given up on Fairtrade certification are using the resources that have been freed up to focus on diversifying their sources of income, growing other crops as well as coffee. This is a positive change where farmers are more independent and have been able to develop local markets for their produce.

To remain relevant, Fairtrade needs to acknowledge these issues. It has an opportunity to be more accountable to southern farmers and fulfil its rhetoric of providing them sustainable livelihoods. If this does not happen, then farmers around the world will continue to say: "Fairtrade is not Fair!" (Mercado Justo no es Justo!)

Current
CONTROVERSIES

CHAPTER 2

Does Fair Trade Protect the Environment?

Environmental Sustainability: Fair Trade Versus Alternative Consumption

Ashley Overbeek

Ashley Overbeek is a master of science student at Stanford University. She studies Earth systems and sustainability.

The notion of alternative consumption seeks to respond to consumer pressures to create a means whereby consumers are able to influence moral issues through the markets and purchasing decisions. This idea stems from two different factors: one, the disenchantment of consumers in the Global North with the efficacy and transparency of direct aid, and two, the desire to create a reliable emotional and ethical network linking consumers in the Global North, those in developed countries, to producers in the Global South, those in developing countries. Goodman 2004 references this idea of eco-labeling functioning as a type of bridge between the somewhat conventionally opaque supply chain from production to consumption by stating:

> "Fair trade attempts to re-connect producers and consumers economically, politically, and psychologically through the creation of a transnational moral economy. This re-connection is accomplished through material and semiotic commoditization processes that produce fair trade commodities. The semiotic production of these commodities and their traffic in particular 'political ecological imaginaries' is essential to the formation of ethical production-consumption links, acting to also politicize consumption and fair trade eaters" (Goodman, 2004:891).

Alternative consumption, viewed from the perspective of political ecology, is not traditionally seen as a viable, long-

"Examining the Efficacy of Fair Trade and Alternative Consumption on Environmental Sustainability and Human Rights in Developing Countries," Ashley Overbeek, *The Journal of Sustainable Development*, Vol. 13, Iss. 1 (2014), Pp. 165-179, https://consiliencejournal .org/wp-content/uploads/sites/25/2016/09/378-998-2-PB.pdf. Licensed under CC BY 4.0 International.

term solution to resource extraction and labor-related company practices in developing countries. In their book, *Eco-Business: A Big-Brand Takeover of Sustainability*, researchers Dauvergne and Lister argue from the political ecologist lens, stating that the system for enacting change through consumption is inherently flawed, simply because capitalistic consumption fundamentally leads to the depletion of natural resources and the oppression of the working class. Byrant et al continues to support this idea, claiming that alternative consumption is a form of "social and political 'caring at a distance' due to an uncritical acceptance of consumption as the primary basis of action."

Though alternative consumption still subscribes to the capitalistic consumer model, it effectively creates a link between the North and the South, and the increased funds from Fair Trade certified premiums have measurable positive effects on community development in the Global South, as well as the increased environmental regulations resulting from farms that are Rainforest Alliance certified. Raynolds supports this claim by acknowledging that the "Fair Trade movement destabilizes neo-liberal knowledge claims regarding the normalcy of commercial conventions" and pushes a shift in corporate mentality from exploitation of both human and natural resources in developing countries to a more harmonious, mutualistic balance with much more transparency. It is important to note, however, that even the term "Fair Trade" is decidedly a Northern term, and succumbs the Southern producers to the definition of fair as generated by the ideals of the Northern consumers. This consequently creates a group of qualifications based on a Northern standard of "fairness" centered around "collective responsibility and evaluations of societal benefits."

It is perhaps myopic to assume, however, that eco-labeling is merely a product of the viewpoints of consumers in the Global North. Rather, the processes of both Fair Trade and Rainforest Alliance eco-labeling can be partially explained through the "actor network theory" in which the producers, consumers, and processors throughout the supply chain all contribute to the final definition of "sustainability." The actor network theory, as defined by Whatmore, emphasizes the plurality of definitions that are shaped by the multiplicity of stakeholders in the capitalist system as a "social composite of the actions and competences of many actants; an attribute not of a single person or organization but of the number of actants involved in its composition."

The Edenization of the Rainforest and Its Effects on the Focus of Eco-Labeling

Currently, the portrayal of the rainforest through eco-labeling and "green" advertising perpetuates the ideal of a biblically pristine ecosystem, a modern Garden of Eden completely separate from the pollution of human industry. This idea uses spiritual rhetoric to spur consumers to want to "Save the Rainforest" and raises public support about ecological conservation efforts. On the other hand, this portrayal can also be extremely problematic at a fundamental level, heightening the importance of environmental sustainability to the complete eclipse of the need for social reform or human rights accountability at the governmental level.

Though Fair Trade does a good job of bringing social issues in developing countries into the agenda of Northern consumers, it does perpetuate a different type of what Bryant's article references as "Edenic myth-making" in regard to how businesses portray the rainforest to consumers in the North. Fair Trade's Edenization involves the "creation of a 'Third World' ambiance, including music and decor, and the telling of producer stories, through producer store visits, photo and video images, and written narratives on the lives of individual producers" as well as the creation of a pristine natural rainforest completely separate from civilization, ripe with the Western notions of "wilderness."

As seen on the Fair Trade Certified website, personal stories from smiling farmers speaking about how Fair Trade has impacted their lives and communities at an individual level abound, in addition to excerpts stating how the certification has created standards for environmental preservation. This storytelling aspect has been critical to the development of alternative consumption, and has shaped a more emotional, personal bond between consumers in the Global North and producers in the Global South.

[...]

Along the same vein of the biblical, Garden of Eden portrayal of tropical forests in developing countries, in his book "Uncommon Ground: Rethinking the Human Place in Nature," environmental historian William Cronon explores humanity's schizoid relationship with nature, a topic that has been exacerbated by green marketing and alternative consumption. This theory states that wilderness has been elevated to a spiritual experience that consumers feel frees them from the mundane confines of human civilization and traditional societal roles. This viewpoint can be problematic in how Northern consumers view the natural resources of developing countries, and therefore through alternative consumption, these viewpoints can directly shape the agendas of NGOs or the specifications for the certification processes for eco-labeling. For example, when the rainforest is portrayed as an untouched, pristine landscape, consumers in the Global North tend to overlook the need to support the indigenous peoples who call the rainforest home. This in turn can create an apathy towards the plight of indigenous tribes or smallholder farmers, who can be viewed as "outsiders" to the forest ecosystem. In other words, because of Edenization, consumers from the Global North are less sympathetic to farmers and smallholders that are cultivating small parts of the rainforest for sustenance because they are not viewed within the idealized, "trees, animals, and nature" rainforest landscape.

Fair Trade certification, paradoxically, both seeks to change this point of view and yet continues to perpetuate it. Fair Trade highlights the plight of humans in a natural setting, thus weaning perceptions away from untouched wilderness and bringing social turmoil and class conflict into the forefront of the Western consciousness. However, in its approach for community-based funding that gives premiums to co-operative farmers, Fair Trade continues to ignore the existing class issues that are perpetuated by government corruption and the exploitative, wealthy elite. In this way, Fair Trade serves as more of a Band-Aid, albeit a relatively successful Band-Aid, instead of a cure. In its own way, Fair Trade exemplifies the Edenization of developing countries, implying that hard-working small farmers are inhibited only by their meager wages through the exploitation of labor by large, multi-natural agribusiness corporations, and fails to address the system of institutionalized oppression and both geographic and socioeconomic discrimination by the arguably corrupt governments of the developing countries. In this way, Fair Trade certification smartly avoids becoming a politicized matter, and it is still important to note the successes of improving the quality of life for farmers on a more localized, case-by-case level.

[…]

Fair Trade Certification: In Principle and In Practice

The history of Fair Trade began in around the 1960s as a niche, alternative market. Fair Trade products were sold in "world shops," or specialty stores that only carry Fair Trade goods. However, as the years progressed, Fair Trade moved into the mainstream market and into larger scale processing and distribution networks that were accessible to a larger slice of Northern society and popular culture and has been growing ever since. Fair Trade spends a large amount of revenue funding extensive, international marketing programs in order to gain brand recognition for the Fair Trade label and incentivize alternative consumption. Indeed, the current focus of Fair Trade has been coined a "mainstreaming strategy" by Taylor, which seeks to "achieve rapid growth in market share by encouraging corporations, governments, major retailers, and other large economic actors to support Fair Trade." In many ways, this approach has allowed for a large expansion of the Fair Trade market, as sales had reached over US$700 million by the end of 2003 according to Murray et al. Fair Trade reported over US$5 billion in sales revenue in 2013.

As defined by Murray et al, "The Fair Trade movement is an effort to link socially and environmentally conscious consumers in the North with producers engaged in socially progressive and environmentally sound farming in the South. It is an attempt to build more direct links between consumers and producers that provide the latter with greater benefits from the marketing of their products than conventional production and trade have allowed, while breaking down the traditional alienation of consumers from the products they purchase." Currently, the Fair Trade certification abides by five major tenets, as indicated from the Fair Trade USA website: (1) access to credit; (2) guaranteed prices; (3), environmental sustainability; (4) labor right; and (5) community development. The posited requirements and their effectiveness in practice are discussed in detail below.

Through the access to credit requirement, buyers are required to offer a line of credit to farmers, allowing them to invest in farm improvements and sustainable infrastructure. However it is unclear how much money is actually loaned and utilized by producers in the Global South. Taylor reports "Participants' access to credit has improved, largely due to FLO's pre-financing requirements" while Lyon critiques the failure of the access to credit in practice because "many cooperative members find it difficult to repay their loans to the cooperative, in turn making it difficult for the group to repay its bank loans."

The guaranteed price is applied through an economic price floor that represents the cost of sustainable production. The international community, not Fair Trade itself, sets this objective cost. This price floor guarantees that farmers will be paid the cost of sustainable production, regardless of market volatility. In the case of coffee, prices have fluctuated so much in 2002 that the guaranteed price represented "as much as double the conventional market price." Some argue, however, that a price floor incentivizes overproduction, flooding the market and even lowering the market price. In addition, the guaranteed price could potentially trap producers in the Fair Trade certification, offering the only means for producers to turn a profit or maintain afloat in an inflated and inefficient market.

In regard to environmental sustainability, for its criteria and/or conditions, Fair Trade prohibits the use of genetically modified organisms, most toxic agrochemicals, and promotes the active conservation of soil, forest, and water resources. These standards are enforced through an audit system, where an independent third-party auditor surveys participating farms for compliance. Though still somewhat nebulous of requirements, measurable results are seen as "small producers are now adopting more environmentally friendly farming techniques to improve the quality of their coffee beans." Fair Trade also demands that no certified farms use child labor, forced labor, or allow workplace discrimination. If child labor or forced labor is discovered during the auditing process, the child or forced laborer will be immediately removed and taken to a safe location. As for workplace discrimination, Fair Trade's most measurable effect has been to improve gender equality at a local level, allowing "some women producers to take greater control of their lives, and not be afraid to participate in decision making both within their cooperative and household."

Perhaps one of the most unique aspects of the Fair Trade policy is its commitment to community development by providing a premium given directly to the farming co-operatives. According to Fair Trade USA's website: "Since 1998, Fair Trade USA and its partners have enabled Fair Trade farmers to earn more than $114 million in community development premiums." This money is put toward a nebulous description of "community development." A representative of Fair Trade elaborated that there is no specific suite of guidelines established by Fair Trade for community development. Rather, the community and the farming co-operative work together to address the specific needs of the community, whether it be paying for the medical treatment of an elderly resident or building a well to bring more accessible water to a village. This flexibility allows individuals in the community to use the money to enact change identified at a local level, which is a much more pragmatic approach than the traditional philanthropic remote instruction, or top-down external oversight.

In this way, Fair Trade addresses the complaint raised by Bryant, who stated that alternative consumption is a mechanism for "caring at a distance." True, consumers are still not directly affecting the communities when they pay the price premium, but this type of spending autonomy to the producers is a much more successful and revolutionary method of exchange. Though the price premium is technically absorbed by the processors, the prices of Fair Trade products are typically higher than traditional non-Fair Trade products, though "consumers are willing to pay higher premiums for coffee labeled as fair trade." Indeed, it is because of the way that Fair Trade is marketed, and the anecdotal advertising strategy which builds a network of transparency from individual producer to individual consumer, that consumers in the Global North are willing to pay a higher premium for a product that they feel directly impacts producers in the Global South. Taylor elaborates on the emotional rhetoric that induces alternative consumption: "This willingness to pay is supported by the building of direct personal ties between Northern consumers and Southern producers." Allowing the community to exercise localized control over how the premium money is spent has had definite success in poverty alleviation, being spent largely "by producer organizations to be invested in crop quality and infrastructure improvements or community projects such as schools and health services."

[…]

Fair Trade Certification as a Tool for Positive Social Change and Environmental Regulation

Conversely, Fair Trade has been seen as an important step in poverty alleviation and environmental protection in developing countries, especially from an economic perspective. It has been documented extensively that producers in the Global South have received additional income from participating in Fair Trade certification. Indeed, "the incomes of most small coffee producers had doubled since their entry into the fair trade market."

Consequentially, this increased revenue has dramatically increased the quality of life for the co-operatives and their surrounding communities, as "many small producers illustrated changes in their lives by referring to greater economic stability and security, in addition to identifying material changes. Some significant improvements they reported included the following: the use of electricity instead of fuel wood, better nutrition, physical improvements to their home, the ability to pay for their children's education and to buy uniforms, shoes, and books, the ability to purchase a vehicle and install a telephone in their home, and the ability to improve the condition of their farm, including purchasing inputs such as organic fertilizer, machinery, and other equipment, and hiring help."

There has also been a noticeable "spillover-effect," as mentioned previously, where not only the farming co-operatives that are in direct contact with Fair Trade benefit, but also their extended families and outlying communities through their interactions with the members of the farming co-operative. As a case study in coffee production confirms, "Fair Trade has provided increased economic and social stability to participants, and greater access to technical training. This in turn has led to improvements in the quality of small-producer coffee and higher productivity. Farmers' families have also benefited, for instance through greater access to education for their children."

As means of production, location, and culture among co-operatives can vary slightly at a case-by-case basis, levels of success for Fair Trade can also vary. However, on the whole, "all the cooperatives participating in Fair Trade have clearly reaped significant benefits from the experience, which has improved the well-being of thousands of small-scale farmers in Mexico and Central America."

Moving Forward: The Future of Alternative Consumption and Fair Trade Certification

As Fair Trade continues to grow as a presence in the farming communities of developing countries, it has several areas of improvement. To revisit the drawbacks of Fair Trade, one of its weakest areas appears to be its lack of ability to address the needs voiced by the Southern producers themselves, or to even provide a reliable medium for producers to provide feedback or provide input on certification standards. This is especially tenuous as Fair Trade becomes more mainstream in the Global North, and must increasingly balance the needs of their profit-driven capitalistic corporations and the requirements of philanthropic environmental and social justice through alternative consumption. Steps that can be taken to improve alternative consumption and Fair Trade certification's sustainability include industry changes as well as political changes.

Fair Trade as an organization can invest in creating more reciprocal channels of communication, allowing for open or even direct exchange of thoughts and ideas from the Global South producers to the Global North consumers. In addition, Fair Trade can focus on creating a system that relies on more producer input to create the certification standards, perhaps even varying the standards based on country or region. On the policy end, both the governments in the Global North and those in the Global South can work together to promote sustainability. The Fair Trade model that has been discussed previously in this paper is fairly straightforward. In this way, this structure can be adopted by governments in both producing and consuming countries, creating national or international legislation to promote price floors on food staples, as well as adding a government tax on certain food products which would fund community development in rural farms and plantations.

Conclusion

The most difficult aspect surrounding the efficacy of Fair Trade certification on environmental sustainability and human rights in developing countries is the variability between different countries, sizes and locations of farming co-operatives, and the crops being produced. Generalizing the successes or drawbacks of Fair Trade as a whole fails to examine the specific traits unique to these extremely diverse areas.

However, in certain aspects, Fair Trade as a governing principle can be analyzed critically and applied to the concept of alternative consumption as a whole. Although it is true that inherently alternative consumption perpetuates the flaws within the market system by subscribing, and therefore conforming to a degree, to the neo-liberal capitalistic culture it is fighting against, alternative consumption also provides a necessary bridge between traditional capitalistic culture and a radically outside-of-market-based solution. Alternative consumption commits to "operating both 'in and against the market', aiming to use the market to transform the market."

Specifically with Fair Trade, Murray et al deems Fair Trade a mechanism that has become "a dynamic and successful dimension of an emerging counter-tendency to the neo-liberal globalization regime."

Alternative consumption and Fair Trade create a link between the producers in the Global South and consumers in the Global North, allowing a personal, albeit sometimes one-sided, relationship to develop, shortening the supply chain and creating more transparency in the traditionally opaque and oppressive global market system. The willingness of consumers to pay the Fair Trade premium, which has made significant documented effects on poverty alleviation and environmental conservation in developing countries, has been ushered in by the personal, anecdotal marketing that is used to promote alternative consumption, but can also shape certification requirements to a Northern ideal. Taylor elaborates, stating, "Fair Trade objects to the abstraction of the market as a depersonalized mechanism operating outside of social institutions and cultural values. It recognizes that economic activity is a social activity invested by humans with social and cultural meaning." One of the biggest concerns for Fair Trade is the need to include producers in the decision-making processes while the expansion of the organization creates the potential for even more influence from multi-national distributing corporations. However, overall, alternative consumption has been an important factor in improving workers' conditions and outcomes—both socially and environmentally—within the communities in developing countries.

Fair Trade Means Protecting the Environment

Fair Trade USA

Fair Trade USA is a nonprofit organization and certifier of fair trade goods.

When people think of Fair Trade, they might think of fair prices for farmers, better labor standards, or maybe even safe working conditions—but what people often forget about is that Fair Trade is equally invested in protecting the environment. Fair Trade not only helps improve farmers' living and working conditions, but also helps them become better stewards of the land. Farmers who struggle to make ends meet are often forced to engage in cheap agricultural practices that compromise surrounding ecosystems.

We at Fair Trade USA believe that in order to improve producers' living and working conditions, their environment must also be clean and healthy.

Strict Environment Standards

Rigorous environmental standards encourage farmers to better protect their delicate ecosystems and reduce the use of harmful chemicals. Here are a few examples of the environmental standards that farms must comply with in order to become Fair Trade Certified:

- Soil and Water: Enhance soil by applying sustainable irrigation practices such as crop rotation; source water sustainably and reduce water use over time
- Biodiversity and Carbon Emissions: Report current benefits and future goals for ecosystems and current methods of carbon emission reductions
- GMOs: Use of GMOs are strictly prohibited

"Why Fair Trade Means Protecting the Environment, Too," Fair Trade USA, April 30, 2012. Reprinted by permission.

- Agrochemicals: Handle agrochemicals safely and minimize their use
- Pests and Waste: Develop sustainable and safe management plans for pests and waste through farmer education

Fair Trade and Organic

Fair Trade and organic certifications are complementary and both show a profound commitment by farmers to environmental responsibility. While Fair Trade Certification does not require organic certification, it does support organic farming with training for producers and a higher price incentive for organic products.

In fact, many producers invest their Fair Trade premium funds in organic certification, which has led to outstanding results: over half (62 percent) of all Fair Trade imports into the United States are also organic, and 52 percent of all Fair Trade producer organizations world-wide hold organic certificates. Ultimately, reaching for these standards encourages the production of goods that benefit you, farming communities and the earth.

A Benchmark for Quality

By adhering to strict Fair Trade standards, farmers are not only able to make great strides in environmental sustainability, but also in the quality of their products. With the Fair Trade premium for community investment, farmers can spend more time and money on things like environmental education, training, quality testing and equipment efficiency. Through the development of sustainable growing and harvesting practices, quality crops are produced at minimal cost to our fragile ecosystem. Here are some inspiring environmental impact projects that were made possible through Fair Trade.

Environmental Education

CoopeTarrazú is a coffee farming cooperative located in the central mountains of San Marcos de Tarrazú, which is perhaps the most famous coffee-growing region in Costa Rica. In 2006, CoopeTarrazú established the Coffee Culture Quality of Life Sustainability Plan to track their environmental impact, implement better practices, and create a culture of environmental respect among members and children. Using the Fair Trade premium, CoopeTarrazú has developed a program that provides trainings, capacity building, and environmental leadership to its members. The key to their program is their focus on raising awareness of ecosystems through a strong educational curriculum for both adults and children.

> "Before, my son never used gloves while he worked. But through the program he learned to protect himself while applying any agricultural inputs. For that I am so glad." —William Naranjo Barrantes, Board Member of CoopeTarrazú Cooperative.

Sustainable Agriculture Project
Associação dos Costas, Brazil

Associação dos Costas is an association of small-scale coffee farmers located in the state of Minas Gerais in southeastern Brazil. Thanks to Fair Trade, Associação dos Costas has developed an Environmental Impact Management project, which is an investigative assessment of the sustainable use, storage and control of agrochemicals on their Brazilian farms. The project resulted in the reduction of glyphosate use, incentives for the rational use of fertilizers and soil remediation, a complete overhaul of chemical storage, increased monitoring of crops, recycling campaigns for the return of empty containers of chemicals and the implementation of land conservation initiatives.

Within two years of implementing the project, the coffee farmers of the Cooperativa Dos Produtores de Café Especial de Boa Esperança Ltda are now using more sustainable inputs and techniques in almost all of their production.

> "Today I am conscious of the environment. I am aware that in doing so, I am improving my quality of life and my family's quality of life. I feel proud to participate in the association. I am valued as a producer and am making new friends and acquiring new knowledge about sustainable agriculture."
> —Antonio Fernandes, Associação dos Costas Member

How Sustainability in Indonesian Coffee Production Is Strengthening Local Communities

Commons Abundance Network

The Commons Abundance Network is a learning network designed to share information about social and ecological threats, connect advocates, and empower change.

There are millions of coffee farmers worldwide who depend on the profits of their hard work to provide for their families. The vast majority of coffee farming is in tropical and developing countries on relatively small farms. Cooperatives can serve to improve livelihoods of farmers as well as promote sustainable agricultural practices. Like labor unions, they can strengthen farmers through unity. NGOs and fair trade organizations can also help to replace exploitative global market relationships between producers and consumers by more ethical practices that provide greater economic benefits to coffee producers. Fair Trade, and eco friendly contracts ensure certain standards are met in the production of coffee beans. Standards are regulated by certification from organizations and companies like UTZ, Rain Forest Alliance, or Max Havelaar. These economic connections are promoting environmentally sustainable practices that do not violate human rights and empower farmers to generate income.

Contexts Within NORA

Relationships to Needs

Sustainable agriculture seeks to improve livelihoods of small scale agriculturalists while promoting environmentally friendly practices of agriculture. Unique forms of agriculture using coffee like inter-cropping or agro-forestry can generate income while also creating food security. It is necessary to reconnect small scale agriculturalists with their land, their environment can be utilized to improve their livelihoods. This article addresses the needs of small scale agriculturalists and also the need for creative alternatives in the global market and agricultural production.

Relationships to Organizational Forms

The goal in sustainable coffee production is essentially based on creating vital non-exploitive links between producers and consumers. Cooperatives unite and empower small scale agricultural communities, they allow farmers to work with one another and gain power through unity. Fair Trade organizations are also enabling social mobility in a global market which has historically been exploitive. These organizational forms are creating new connections between consumers and producers while empowering small scale farmers.

Relationships to Resources

Free Trade standards and Cooperatives are organizations that can promote sustainable agriculture that does not harm the environment with unsustainable extraction of natural resources. Sustainable coffee production provides an alternative to extractive regimes which have degraded the environment. Organic and sustainable forms of coffee production such as agro-forestry can help to preserve the environment and biodiversity of natural ecosystems. Cooperatives also enable agriculturalists to utilize their land to generate income while not harming the land.

Information on Coffee

Coffee is widely consumed and is in fact the second largest traded commodity after petroleum. Consumption of the beverage is highest in the United States and Europe. Coffee is cultivated in high altitude tropical places. *Rubiaceae* is the scientific name for the coffee family which has 500 genera and 6000 species, but 99% of the coffee produced in the world comes from two different species:

Arabica and Robusta. *Coffea arabica* is the higher quality bean of the two species. It originates from the Ethiopian Highlands and is grown best between the elevations 1,500-2,000 meters. *Coffea canephora*, better known as robusta coffee is usually used for cheaper blends of coffee and instant coffee.

Several steps are included in the creation of coffee; first the beans are cultivated, harvested, and then processed. Beans are also roasted to distinct flavor and transported all across the world. Coffee is made from berries which are picked when they are ripe, these are referred to as cherries because they resemble cherries. The picked berries are then processed and dried to get to the bean. When imported, the coffee beans are then roasted according to the desired roast before being grounded and brewed to make coffee the drink. Green (un-roasted) coffee beans are one of the most traded agricultural commodities in the world.[1]

Coffee cultivation started in Ethiopia and Yemen. Arab traders started producing and trading coffee in the 14th century. Then at the turn of the 16th century in 1595, the Dutch arrived in Indonesia. Soon after their arrival the Dutch East India Company was established in 1602, and they then started the production of coffee as a commercial crop in Indonesia. The term "Java" refers to the Indonesian island where a large portion of coffee was cultivated. Java is the most populated of the Indonesian islands yet it still plays an important part in food production. Plantation systems were a component of the economic system created by the Dutch. Today production can vary between large company plantations and small scale cultivators under fair trade contracts. Much of the sustainably grown coffee and fair trade certified coffee is shipped to Europe, especially Germany. There is also an increasing market in the United States and Canada for fair trade and organic coffee.

Along with rising concerns over coffee cultivation and its impacts on the environment, organically grown coffee is on the rise and is being demanded in the global market. Mass produced coffee can have negative impacts on the environment through residues which are toxic. There are two important certifications that are used for coffee, Fair trade and Organic coffee. Fair Trade is a term claiming that a coffee product was produced and marketed on an ethically set standard that does not violate human welfare. Organic coffee is a term used to describe coffee that was produced without pesticides and herbicides. Furthermore there are additional certifications that claim that a coffee product was produced without harming the environment, e.g. Rain Forest Alliance. It is important to note that both of these terms can vary in their exact definitions, for each certification may require different standards to be met. Small cooperatives can serve as environmentally friendly alternatives to mass produced coffee processing. Fair Trade organizations can also be useful for ensuring that small scale cultivators of coffee are being paid and treated ethically.

Background of Indonesia

Indonesia is a large and diverse nation made up of approximately 17,508 islands inhabited by 253,609,643 in 2014 according to the CIA World Factbook.[2] There are five main islands that are home to most of the total Indonesian population Sumatra, Kalimantan, Sulawesi, Irian Jaya and Java. With its lush tropical climate, Indonesia has diverse forms of agriculture such as rice, banana, rubber, coffee, and many other forms of cultivation. The most popular form of agriculture in Indonesia is *Sawah*, which is wet rice farming, rice is the staple food for Indonesians. The landscape varies greatly from marshes, to high elevation rainforests, it is in areas of high elevation where the best quality of coffee can be grown. About half of the country is covered by rain forests, although that number is dropping as a result of rapid deforestation. The rapid deforestation is a result of unsustainable agriculture, logging, and mining. Deforestation has not only degraded the environment, but has endangered the rich bio-diversity of animals like the Sumatran tiger, Javan rhinoceros, orangutan, and Sumatran elephant.

Indonesia has undergone much political change over its history: Dutch colonization, Japanese colonialism, the first independent government under Sukarno, who was topple by Suharto with the backing of the CIA. Suharto introduced neo-liberal policies (until he resigned in 1998 during the Asian economic crisis), which opened the door for large corporations to extract natural resources unsustainably at the cost of human welfare and environment. With its massive population of over a quarter billion people, it is said that the Indonesian economy is growing; in 2010 it was reported to be the 27th biggest exporting country in the world (though one might expect a higher ranking from the fourth most populous country in the world).[3] At the same time, there is growing poverty in Indonesia. According to a report in 2016, 39 million (18% of the total 220 million in Indonesia) are classified as poor by the Indonesian government's statistics bureau. 75% of those classified as poor earn their living from agriculture. This draws attention to the need to empower farmers in Indonesia to generate income and improve livelihoods, while practicing agriculture sustainably without damaging the environment.

Government Policies of Land Use

Suharto, the New Deal, & the Extractive Regime

Politics are intertwined not only with human welfare, but ecological factors as well. The New Order was the term attached to Indonesian President Suharto's economic policy. Following the coup against leftist Indonesian leader Sukarno, Suharto established an extractive regime based on large-scale, unsustainable exploitation of resources such as timber, petroleum, oil palm, and rubber, that brought Indonesian products into the global market. The Indonesian government has encouraged large foreign corporations to invest in Indonesia, leading to much intensification of extraction of natural resources. The intensified extraction of natural resources not only harms the environment but also human welfare by seizing indigenous lands, violating human rights, and creating large discrepancies of wealth in society. Because Suharto's legacy continues today, it is necessary to advocate for policies that empower disenfranchised people while preserving the environment. The goal is to achieve harmony between ecology and culture.

Alternatives to the Extractive Regime

Extractive regimes in Indonesia have yielded environmental degradation, exploitation of labor, and mass dislocation of peoples from their native lands; alternatives must be found and practiced. There is a great need to sustainably manage the extraction of natural resources in order to preserve the environment while empowering the livelihoods of local peoples. Agricultural coffee co-operatives could be a way to provide marginalized rural people with the ability to generate income and utilize natural resources to meet their needs. Coffee is the 2nd most traded commodity in the world, behind oil, and a large portion of the world's coffee comes from Indonesia. According to US Department of Agriculture date from 2010-11, Indonesia was the fourth largest producer of coffee in the world, producing 9.3 million bags, each bag weighing 60 kilograms. The World Mapper also reports Indonesia as the world's fourth largest producer, producing an annual average of 7.4 million 60 kg bags of coffee beans during the early 2000's. However many of these beans are the lesser quality *Robusta* beans which are cultivated for instant coffee. While vastly outproduced by the world's largest producer, Brazil, that produced 54.5 million bags in 2010-11, Indonesia still produces a significant share of the world total.

Fair trade movements and co-operatives are re-linking coffee producers and consumers, which benefits cultivators financially while promoting sustainability. Contemporary consumers are starting to make two demands for ethically produced coffee. Firstly for environmentally friendly practices such as modest use of fertilizers, pesticides, water and energy. Secondly for human rights such as education for children of coffee farmers instead of being put to work, decent labor rights, housing, healthcare, and empowerment for farm workers. A substantial portion of the world's consumers are demanding that specialty coffee beans be grown ethically and not mass produced. This analysis shows how methods of coffee co-operatives and production can create greater abundance and create social mobility for rural and lower classes of society.

Coffee Cooperatives in Indonesia

Cooperatives

Sustainable practices are an answer to both environmental degradation and violations of human rights, but these practices must be properly and strategically executed. Cooperatives enable farmers to collaborate with one another, pooling their resources and strengthening themselves as a collective to produce abundance of cultivated crops. They not only help producers control the land, but also help farmers to get better prices for their produce. Uniting farmers gives them greater collective bargaining powers. Furthermore large buyers prefer to buy in large lots that save them time and money. Cultivate.coop is a wiki which provides information on how to start an agricultural cooperative. Peer learning between farmers groups can share awareness, knowledge, technique, and spread ecological literacy.

Land is the key for subsistence, cooperatives enable farmers to control their local resources. *Adat* is an Indonesian term that refers to indigenous customary law regarding how to cooperatively deal with resources, its main goal is harmony between peoples and place. Original accumulation (also known as primitive accumulation, refers to the origins of capital and how classes are created between those who possess and don't possess) separates farmers from their land and subsistence, in part by undermining traditional norms such as the Indonesian *adat*. Farmers would often lose their land to large encroaching corporations, for example an oil palm plantation may intimidate farmers into selling their land for a far less than fair price, or not even recognize that they have rights to the land. Often an extractive regime government overlooks violations of civil rights by corporations with the idea that corporations that intensify production will be better for the economy. Empowering farmers to control their land and resources serves as a way to avert original accumulation, and to ensure that economic activity actually serves the needs of the people rather than enriching distant shareholders.

Sustainable Practices

Sustainable agriculture seeks to make the best use out of nature's goods and services, of knowledge and skills of farmers, of people's collective capacity to work together to solve problems. It is the goal for coffee cultivators to implement agricultural techniques that do not harm the environment, while ensuring that farmers are generating income in ways that are sustainable, which in turn empowers and creates social mobility for farmers.

Two useful techniques that can be used in sustainable agriculture are agro-forestry and intercropping. Agro-forestry refers to combining tree crops with another crop; this can easily be applied to coffee which naturally grows best under the shade of the rainforest canopy. Intercropping is the practice of growing two or more crops in proximity. The most common goal of intercropping is to produce a greater yield on a given piece of land by making use of resources that would otherwise not be utilized by a single crop. Shade grown coffee refers to *Arabica* coffee that is grown in the shade; it is a viable alternative to deforestation. *Robusta* coffee beans don't require to be grown in the shade and can grow in tropical lowlands. Instead of deforestation, forests can be preserved as sources of shade under which coffee can be grown. Organic shade grown coffee doesn't degrade the land, it allows coffee to grow in its natural environment and reduce soil erosion. Leaf litter from the canopy and coffee plants is good for soil nutrition, while coffee bushes and tree roots help to hold soil in place. This form of coffee production doesn't destroy the rainforest, though it does substantially alter its species composition.

Human Welfare and Contracts

Fair trade certification is used to ensure that farmers are being treated fairly, this includes working conditions, education, and that farmers are being paid a fair amount. Fair trade contracts provide small farming families with enough money to improve their livelihoods by paying a price that is guaranteed to be above a given floor price when market prices are low, and above market prices otherwise. The global market of the coffee bean fluctuates wildly in prices, when the price of beans drop, farmers stop producing coffee, which then leads to an increase in price because of a shortage in coffee production. Contracts guarantee prices that support a stable livelihood, and work outside of the fluctuating market. Contracts under fair trade certification also ensure that products are produced under good working conditions with respect for the environment.

Global Market

Rural people are often marginalized and exploited in the globalized market. A key aspect of coffee cooperatives is making vital connections across the globe by re-linking producers with consumers. Environmental and labor movements find common ground in the fair trade and sustainable coffee movements because these methods both preserve the environment and ensure social justice. The global market can actually be used as a vehicle for empowerment by connecting consumers who want ethically produced coffee with producers. Cooperatives and NGOs serve as the links between producer and consumer, using these links will benefit both environment and human welfare. Fair Trade USA's mission statement is to "…empowering farmers and workers around the world with the business training and capital investment necessary to grow high-quality products that can compete in global markets." Furthermore, Fair Trade USA seeks to link organizations from all areas of the supply chain to maximize impact for producers. Fairtrade standards for coffee act as a safety net against the unpredictable world market. They provide security to coffee producers so that they will get a price that covers their average costs of sustainable production. The standards that Fairtrade International follows for certification are:

- Producer organizations are paid a floor price (Fairtrade Minimum Price) of US 1.40 per pound for Fairtrade certified washed Arabica and US 1.35 for unwashed Arabica, or the market price, if higher.

- For Fairtrade certified organic coffee an extra minimum differential of US 30 cents per pound is being applied.
- A Fairtrade Premium of US 20 cents (with USD 5 cents earmarked for productivity and quality improvements) per pound is added to the purchase price and is used by producer organizations for social and economic investments at the community and organizational level.
- Fairtrade coffee certification is currently only open to small farmer organizations. Small farmers must be organized in organizations which they own and govern.
- Democratic decision making is required. Everybody has equal right to vote.
- Environmental standards restrict the use of agrochemicals and encourage sustainability.
- Pre-export lines of credit are given to the producer organizations. If requested, up to 60 % of the purchase price should be pre-financed to the producer organizations.
- Trade standards aim to encourage fairer negotiations, clarify the role of price fixing, and reduce speculation

The Fair Trade Organization Max Havelaar, seeks to establish long term contractual relationships between producers and exporters. Exporters pay a guaranteed price under contract, pay a development premium and an advance payment. Max Havelaar monitors working conditions (no forced labor, no child labor, freedom of association and collective negotiation, etc.). Finally, it ensures observance of ecological criteria, including a ban on GMOs (Genetically Modified Organisms). With 23 other national fair trade labeling organizations, Max Havelaar Belgium is a member of FLO International (Fairtrade Labelling Organisations). Fair Trade USA and Max Havelaar are just a couple of examples of fair trade organizations.

Predicaments and Obstacles

Food security exists if people are secure that they will consistently have enough food. Since coffee beans are not a source of food and their harvest may fail, inter-cropping and agro-forestry can increase farmers' food security by providing food even if they cannot sell their coffee. These two techniques are also good for soil nutrition and preventing erosion.

A major obstacle to overcome is creating effective cooperatives and linking these cooperatives with consumers to buy their products. Products also need to be certified that they are ethically made, there are many organizations that provide certification for products. Another obstacle is ensuring that consumers keep buying from the producer and that the production of the product does not harm the environment or violate human rights. Effective agricultural extension of products, technology, and information is important to help keep cooperatives running effectively.

Tad Mutersbaugh found in his research that fair trade and organic certifications need to be rethought together with efforts to assist producer certification. This should be a priority for supporters of sustainable agriculture. Certification can complicate production and labor union organization because it is difficult to balance standards of production and producers interests. Furthermore another challenge Mutersbaugh addressed ("Fighting Standards with Standards," 2005) "The shift to globalized standards has transformed rent relations in ways that benefit certain actors (that is, retailers) and imperil the earnings of others. In brief, globalized standards increase the costs of standards compliance, the full burden of which falls upon immiserated producers, to the point at which farmers see little economic advantage to certified-organic and fair-trade production." A solution to the issue Mutersbaugh, taken from his title, is to fight standards with standards, he proposes that social-accountability standards can be used to certify strong labor and environmental protection standards under a single label. Simply stated, a single-standard system can make complexity of standard certification easier on small scale producers, cooperatives, and unions.

There is some question whether certification standard can help small scale farmers; a study by the The International Institute for Environment and Development investigates whether this system benefits poor and marginalized farmers. These standards do help farmers to reach new markets and learn new skills. However, these practices cost more than what some farmers can afford, this study (Blackmore, et al, 2012) concluded that "These farmers need carefully targeted support from external agencies such as governments, NGOs, the private sector or the certification bodies themselves in order to attain benefits of certification." Strong and ethically managed entities must work hand in hand with small scale farmers with the goal of improving their livelihood, preserving the environment, and creating abundance through this collaboration.

The growing fair trade coffee market has re-linked producers and consumers with a viable alternative to an often exploitative world trade market. Cooperatives have addressed the needs of small scale agriculturalists in Indonesia, it has enabled them to use their land to generate income and improve their livelihoods while preserving the environment. However sometimes the standards of certification create a barrier that some farmers fear they cannot cross. Cooperatives and collaboration are one solution that help to ease the pressures of fair trade standards. Cooperatives help to effectively share knowledge and labor to meet standards and generate income. Cooperatives are transforming communities and protecting the environment; promoting agricultural techniques that are sustainable and do not harm the environment.

Notes

[1] Mussatto, Solange I.; Machado, Ercília M. S.; Martins, Silvia; Teixeira, José A. (2011). "Production, Composition, and Application of Coffee & Its Industrial Residues". Food and Bioprocess Technology 4 (5): 661–72.

[2] Information on Indonesia. ASEM Development conference II: Towards an Asia-Europe partnership for sustainable development. 26–27 May 2010, Yogyakarta, Indonesia. ec.europa.eu

[3] http://www.thejakartapost.com/news/2011/06/07/indonesia-rises-27th-biggest-exporter-world-2010.html.

Fair Trade Farmers Work to Protect the Environment

Heather Nicholson

Heather Nicholson is the digital officer for the Fairtrade Foundation in the United Kingdom.

Farmers say climate change is one of the number one threats they face. Millions of farmers around the world who rely on agriculture for their livelihoods are among the worst affected.

Environmental protection is ingrained in Fairtrade. To sell Fairtrade products, farmers have to improve soil and water quality, manage pests, avoid using harmful chemicals, manage waste, reduce their greenhouse gas emissions and protect biodiversity. Here are eight ways Fairtrade supports farmers to survive climate change threats and reduce their own carbon footprint.

Reforestation Projects

Many Fairtrade co-operatives choose to invest their Fairtrade Premium in reforestation projects. Planting trees on cleared, degraded land prevents soil erosion and reduces climate change by binding and storing carbon dioxide. The trees also improve biodiversity, protect soils, and provide a habitat for indigenous wildlife. Sireet OEP in East Africa planted 150k trees in a year alone.

Prohibiting Harmful Agrochemicals

Fairtrade prohibits the use of certain agrochemicals that are harmful to the environment and encourages farmers to reduce their use of pesticides.

Vietnam is known worldwide for exporting large volumes of coffee, and farmers often suffer the negative environmental impact of using chemical pesticides. Eakiet, one of the first Fairtrade

"8 Ways Fairtrade Farmers Protect the Environment," by Heather Nicholson, Fairtrade Foundation, June 5, 2018. Reprinted by permission.

cooperatives in Vietnam, is based in a region enriched with natural resources and several national parks. Through training, the co-operative has stopped using pesticides and herbicides. If there is an outbreak of insects, they use high-pressure water to remove them. They continuously weed and prune their trees during the rainy season when the risk of pests and disease increases.

Growing Trees and Crops Together

Growing trees and several kinds of crops together increases families' farm yields and, with it, their access to food and income.

Trees provide shade for crops and when the leaves fall and decompose, they make the soil more fertile and crops get a better yield. It also enables diversified food production and helps to improve families' intake of nutritional food, which is especially important for persons living with HIV.

Climate Change Adaptation

Fairtrade promotes training on climate change mitigation for farmers. For example, some training offers advice on switching to environmentally friendly practices, such as developing nutrient-rich soils that support healthy plants and encouraging wildlife to help control pests and diseases.

In 2013, organic banana producers from Piura in Peru were hit by a severe outbreak of the "red rust thrips" pest, believed to be triggered by climate change. This affected 40 percent of farms and reduced exports by 30 percent. In partnership with a German retailer, a local university and a banana co-operative, Fairtrade implemented a project to train farmers to find solutions to the outbreak, such as increasing biodiversity and using local plants to repel the insects. By the end of the project, red rust thrips were under control and the amount of discarded crop was at a minimum.

Wildlife Conservation Projects

Coobana Co-operative in Panama uses a slice of the Fairtrade Premium they earn from selling bananas to protect endangered turtles that hatch on beaches nearby. With this money, they invest in a local NGO, patrol the beaches at night during hatching season and clean up the shoreline. River-dwelling manatees have also won the support of Coobana Co-operative. A separate fund helps protect and feed the local population of manatees who suffer from the high levels of pollution found in the rivers.

Fairtrade Carbon Credits

Carbon credits in essence are tonnes of carbon dioxide that have been prevented from entering or have been removed from the atmosphere. Companies can purchase credits to take responsibility for the emissions they produce. These credits can be earnt by smallholder farmers through sustainability projects such as reforestation and switching to biogas stoves. The funding for these projects is covered by the carbon credits and the farmers receive a Fairtrade Premium.

Switching to Green Energy Fuels

Deforestation for firewood is a big issue in Ethiopia. The rapid deforestation is directly related to poverty. As people need to sustain their livelihoods, 46 percent of felling is due to daily energy needs. Traditionally, many people cook over an open-fire, which is both harmful to the environment and women's health. The use of solid fuel open fires and leaky stoves causes an estimated 4.3 million premature deaths each year. Smoke kills more people than TB, HIV/ AIDS and malaria combined. Oromia Co-operative in Ethiopia has taken part in the carbon credit initiative to purchase biogas stoves.

This project equipped 10,000 coffee farmers with 20,000 efficient cookstoves. The new stoves reduce the use of firewood by 50 percent, the release of harmful soot particles by 24-45 percent, and carbon emissions up to 70 percent. Powered by cow dung, these biogas stoves create by-products which can be used as organic fertiliser on the farm.

Reducing Water Usage

COOCAFE co-operative in Costa Rica spent some of their Fairtrade Premium on a new water treatment system in processing plants. This new system has reduced water use from 2,000-3,000 litres per 225 kg of coffee to 200 litres.

When you buy Fairtrade, you are supporting farmers through the often devastating impact of climate change.

Produce Grown Overseas Increases Our Carbon Footprint

Annie Kelly

Annie Kelly writes for the Guardian *and the* Observer. *She is currently the editor of the* Guardian's Modern Day Slavery in Focus *series and has won several awards for her writing.*

Fairtrade has been a major player in pushing ethical consumerism into the mainstream and on to the high street. Ten years ago we all knew that poor workers in developing countries weren't getting a fair deal for producing the food we were eating, but few were reflecting this in their purchasing decisions. Now that is changing.

Fairtrade sales are up by 40% year on year and last year the Fairtrade market was estimated to be worth more than £450m. "One of Fairtrade's biggest victories so far has been to get consumers aware of their role and responsibility in the global food chain," says Ian Bretman, deputy director of the Fairtrade Foundation. "And this has put far greater pressure on retailers to start being more transparent about the social and environmental impacts our consumerism is having across the world."

Fairtrade has always stood for clear social principles and values. But in our world of melting glaciers and burning forests, ethical consumerism is becoming as much about environmental as social concerns.

New research by the Co-operative Group into the areas of primary concerns for more than 100,000 of its members and shoppers shows environmental impact (22%) is almost as much of a priority as ethical trading (27%). This concern is reflected in the boom in "eco" labelling schemes and products that now sit alongside the Fairtrade label on UK supermarket shelves.

Carbon Footprints and Food Miles

With air travel fast becoming the pariah of the environmental movement, the pressure for businesses to reduce their carbon footprint has persuaded supermarkets, including Marks & Spencer, to introduce air mile and carbon-footprint stickers on airfreighted foods.

Go into a branch of Marks & Spencer and you'll find that more than 100 different food products, such as beans, mangetout and strawberries, carry a sticker telling shoppers that it has been airfreighted into our shopping baskets.

But is the growing preoccupation with food miles a problem for Fairtrade? "A potential problem that things like airfreight and carbon emission labelling schemes present for Fairtrade food producers is the misconception that most imported food, including Fairtrade, is flown in," says Tara Garnett, founder of the Food Climate Research Network. In fact, Garnett says, out of 3,000 Fairtrade-certified products sold in the UK, only one—roses from Kenya—are airfreighted in, and this one product accounts for just 0.8% of all Fairtrade imports.

With the other 99.2% of Fairtrade products entering the UK by ship, which is a relatively low carbon emitter, in 2005 the international transportation of Fairtrade products to the UK was responsible for just 0.03% of UK food mile emissions and 0.001% of total UK carbon emissions.

The Soil Association, the body that certifies food with the "organic" label, has completed a lengthy consultation programme around just this issue. It concludes that it will not be putting airfreight labels on its flown-in organic certified products because it fears it will feed misconceptions among UK consumers. Garnett agrees: "You simply can't judge how ethical a food product is by its food miles," she says. "Most environmental damage in the food chain occurs at the agricultural rather than at the food stages and, at the moment, the contribution of food air freighting to climate change is minor."

Garnett points out that, as a sector, the UK's meat and dairy industries are by far much larger emitters of carbon than fruit and vegetables flown in from overseas. You might think you're being green by buying locally sourced lamb from Wales, but in fact that lamb will have travelled a huge distance by road in a heavy, emission-spewing goods vehicle to get into your oven.

"So it's very disingenuous of retailers to try to keep consumers fixated on air miles," she says. "In many ways you could say it's because it's easier for them to focus consumers' attention on that than on whether they're promising to start changing the way they trade with overseas producers."

Brad Hill, Fairtrade strategic development manager at the Co-operative Group, says there is a grim irony to the fact that Fairtrade producers might suffer from a backlash against environmental goods when they themselves are some of the world's lowest emitters.

"You've got to think of the impact on overseas producers and the livelihoods of farmers in developing countries if a blanket position was taken on this view of air miles," says Hill. "Remember that the consumers choosing Fairtrade are largely the same consumers who want to buy organic or help the environment. We have to make sure our ethical consumer base is aware it's possible to shop in a way that both gives a better deal to food producers overseas and benefits the environment."

While products that bear the Fairtrade mark are subject to tight environmental criteria, the movement will have to start increasing its eco credentials if it is to meet the concerns of ethical consumers. "Many of the small producer communities are aware of the need to protect and look after their natural environment," says Bretman. "And our environmental guidelines already mean that Fairtrade food is produced in a way that protects and conserves the natural environment. We just have to get better at passing this message on to consumers."

Natural Bedfellows

Simon Billing, of Fairtrade company Twin, says that Fairtrade and environmental protection are natural bedfellows. "Fifteen years ago, when we talked about giving smallhold farmers' market access and making the Fairtrade proposition work commercially, people laughed in our faces," he says. "Now we've shown that it can work, the movement is moving into discussing environmental issues and how we can best support our producers over the degradation of their natural resources."

Billing believes that Fairtrade is uniquely placed to play an active role in promoting environmental sustainability by building up the movement and giving the farmers the ability to invest in their environment and deal with issues such as decreasing production.

"The farmers we work with are telling us that we are living in an increasingly fragile world, and my vision of Fairtrade in the future is that it will work as a triangle focusing on quality of life, quality of product and quality of the environment," says Billing. "If you denigrate the environment you're putting the livelihoods of those who work the land at risk. The challenge for the movement is to show consumers that by helping our producers, they are helping the environment at the same time."

The Dark Side of Coffee: An Unequal Social and Environmental Exchange

Alexander J. Myers

Alexander J. Myers is a PhD student in the department of sociology at the University of Kansas. His research focuses on the coffee industry's environmental and social impacts throughout the world.

The humble coffee bean is one of the most important and actively traded commodities in the world. It doesn't take more than a glance at American coffee consumption stats to understand why.

In a 2015 Gallup poll, 64% of Americans reported drinking at least one cup of coffee per day and 2.7 on average. The United States imports about 2.8 billion pounds of green coffee every year, and Americans consume just over nine pounds of coffee per capita annually.

If you're anything like me, your morning coffee is a necessity, so early in my graduate career I decided to do a little research on it. I found a fascinating and somewhat disturbing story encompassing ecology, economics, globalization and finance—one that all coffee drinkers should know about.

Out with Shade-Grown

Beginning in the 1970s, many Latin American coffee farmers began to convert their farms to what is called "technified" production systems. In response to disease outbreaks in Brazil during the early '70s, large growers began to search for new, heartier coffee varietals.

Encouraged by local and national governments—along with development aid agencies like USAID—many of these farmers began to cut down the trees that create the canopy under which coffee has traditionally been grown and plant in their place varietals specially bred to grow in full sun. Those selected were heartier and more resistant to disease and pests—and were also less affected by the application of chemical fungicides.

By the end of the 1990s, sun or reduced-shade cultivation systems accounted for almost 70% of Colombia's land area devoted to coffee and 40% of Costa Rica's.

These technified plots can be up to five times more productive than shade systems, but also come with significant environmental consequences. Shade coffee farms have proven to harbor some of the highest levels of biodiversity, particularly for insects and migratory birds, among all agro-ecosystems (those whose products are used for human consumption).

Furthermore, a recent study found that, from seed to mug, each cup of coffee uses about 140 liters of "virtual water," which takes into account water used for irrigation, processing and shipping, as well as for consumption. This figure is significantly higher for coffee grown in full-sun versus that grown under shade cover.

Since it's grown out of the more balanced ecosystem of the shaded grove, technified coffee requires much higher levels of chemical pesticides to combat pests. And since technified plants produce so much more coffee and don't have the benefit of using recycled plant matter, farmers need to apply more fertilizer to make up for the loss of soil nutrients from year to year. The application of these chemicals can have detrimental long-term effects on a region's biodiversity and soil health.

Unequal Exchange

At its core, technification applies the industrial-agricultural model to coffee production, and in many ways it has intensified exploitative relationships between coffee consumers in the global North and coffee producers in the global South—what are colloquially called "first-world" and "third-world" countries, respectively.

Social scientists have been studying these lopsided North-South dynamics for well over a century, but the topic has recently been recast with a distinctly "green" bent.

Environmental economists and sociologists have developed the concept of ecologically unequal exchange, which holds that developed countries externalize a significant portion of their "ecological footprint" to developing ones. Put more simply, industrialized countries use the ecological carrying capacity of periphery countries to offset the environmental impact of their own consumption.

Large statistical studies have confirmed this. Sociologist James Rice found that, among lower- and lower-middle-income countries, those with higher proportions of trade export to Northern countries had lower domestic resource consumption net of other factors.

Similarly, his colleague Andrew Jorgenson's study confirms these results, while also adding an interesting finding: that the relationships between Northern importers and Southern exporters became more unequal from 1975 to 2000. More than one-third of the countries in Jorgenson's sample were major coffee exporters, including production giants like Colombia and Brazil and other important players such as Costa Rica, Kenya, Vietnam and Mexico that obtain a significant portion of GDP from coffee export revenues.

Another recent study by sociologist Kelly Austin found that, even after controlling for overall agricultural export-dependence, a country's reliance on coffee exports as a significant share of gross domestic product (GDP) "produces unique and especially harmful patterns [of] deforestation, hunger and schooling in poor nations in comparison to other forms of agricultural production."

Placing coffee at the center of highly unequal trade relationships between North and South, these studies show that commodity coffee production is rife with multiple forms of socioecological exploitation.

Better Way?

Several movements have sprung up to address many of these inequities by raising awareness and offering a more equitable alternative.

Fair trade certification provides economic stability for farmers by providing them a base price for their coffee, requiring unionization or cooperative business structures and encouraging them to adopt more sustainable farming practices. A newer movement, direct trade, has buyers send representatives directly to coffee farms to observe their practices and develop long-term trading relationships.

Both of these tend to return more money to producers and provide them incentives to help lessen their coffee's impact. Yet both depend on consumer demand and center around the willingness (and ability) of affluent Westerners to pay higher prices for their coffee. This demand can dry up quickly, leaving producers with lots of high-quality, expensive coffee that no one wants.

Longer-lasting change will need to come from international agreements and local economic and political changes in the coffee lands themselves. But for now these alternative-trading systems are a step in the right direction to address the socioecological exploitation plaguing the industry today.

Current
CONTROVERSIES

CHAPTER 3

Does Fair Trade Positively Impact Communities?

Fair Trade's Social Impact Varies by Country

Kevin Behne

Kevin Behne is a writer for the Center for Global Prosperity.

The concept of "fair trade" is somewhat nebulous. Different individuals and interest groups have construed the term in very different ways. One of the most common interpretations of fair trade, however, has involved various organizations that advocate fair trade with respect to various products that are imported from emerging economies. For these groups, fair trade encompasses the equitable treatment of producers and workers in developing countries, focusing primarily on labor protection and sustainable development. For an extra cost, consumers or companies may purchase a certified product that grantees a "living wage" and better working conditions. In recent years, this movement has gained quite a significant following, expanding to cover a wide variety of products, including coffee, cocoa, bananas, and textiles.

Fair trade products have seen increasing integration into the global market. Prominent examples include Starbucks and McDonald's decisions to purchase fair trade coffee, Nestle's plan to fair trade certify its chocolate, and Ben & Jerry's ambitious use of fair trade ingredients only. These products have also found their way to store shelves; in the U.S. alone, an estimated 11,000 fair trade products can be found in at least 70,000 stores. In 2010, the products constituted $1.2 billion in retail sales. The fair trade brand can also improve a product's marketability; the Wall Street Journal reported a study in which "fair trade certified" stickers were attached to coffee products in a select number of stores. As it turns out, the stores which had the labels saw a 13% increase in sales of the product, even when the price of the product was raised by $1 a pound.

"Is Fair Trade Actually Fair?" by Kevin Behne, Hudson Institute, The Center for Global Prosperity, July 3, 2012. Reprinted by permission.

There can be little doubt that fair trade products have a certain appeal to consumers, despite their higher costs. But the question must be asked: do fair trade products really help the poor in developing countries? The answer is mixed. For the Salvadorian community of El Guabo, a 600 family farm cooperative that grows bananas, the impact of fair trade has been quite positive. Water quality has drastically improved from a diminished use of chemicals (required for free trade certification), leading to fewer diseases. Social programs, funded by the profits, have given the community improved access to education, healthcare, and conservation.

The movement has also made commendable progress on the issue of gender equality. In many of the countries fair trade is involved in, women face many instances of unequal treatment, discrimination, and harassment. In response, the fair trade movement actively seeks to give women an opportunity to work in non-discriminatory environment. The response has been positive: women hold many leadership roles in many of the cooperatives. In many networks, women represent over 60% of the workforce, working as artisans, farmers, traders, academicians, and professionals. Specialty groups have emerged such as SAME SKY, a fair trade group that makes jewelry, exclusively employing HIV-positive women who were victims of sexual violence during the Rwandan Genocide.

At first glance, fair trade may seem to be a win-win scenario for producers and consumers. A more in-depth examination, however, reveals that there are some distinct drawbacks to fair trade practices. In order to receive fair trade certification, the parties receiving the endorsement, must be a member of a cooperative. Individual farmers and corporations are excluded. The certification process is somewhat expensive: an average-sized organization will pay about $3,300 to apply for the certification and about $1,300 to $2,200 for a biennial renewal. This excludes the infrastructure and labor costs to comply with fair trade standards. Consequentially, the overhead costs diminish the returns: less than 25% of fair trade premiums return to the producers.

While many of the rules and regulations perpetrated by fair trade agreements have sound principles behind them, enforcement of the rules can be somewhat elusive. Although fair trade producers are supposed to adhere to the most stringent environmental standards, they are not always met: an estimated one-fifth of fair trade coffee has been found illegally planted in virgin rainforests. Labor conditions for workers have also been problematic. Because the agreements are made between the cooperatives and the fair trade organizations, the workers that harvest the products are not always afforded adequate protection. In Peru, fair trade coffee growers were caught underpaying seasonal workers. In Burkina Faso, a fair trade cotton supplier for Victoria's Secret was found exploiting child labor, a direct violation of the agreement. Undoubtedly, many other scandals within the fair trade movement have yet to see the light of day. But the biggest losers are the farmers excluded from fair trade labeling. As previously mentioned, farmers cannot receive certification unless they organize into larger cooperatives. The farmers unable to gain certification are left with a stigmatized brand, giving them a competitive disadvantage. This has been particularly problematic given that fair trade agreements are primarily given to middle income countries. The top four countries (Mexico, Columbia, Peru, and South Africa) have an average GDP per capita of $4,790. By contrast, the 13 nations with only one fair trade producer have a GDP per capita of $2,807. The phenomena is compounded by the "Honeypot Effect": it is tempting for governments, NGOs, and private organizations to give financial support to fair trade cooperatives that are already well managed. Focusing resources in such places may produce immediate results, but it does divert assistance away from the farmers with greater needs outside the cooperatives.

Altruistic as their motives may be, the fair trade movement has not produced entirely uniform benefits for producers and farmers in developing countries. Whether the costs outweigh the benefits remains to be seen.

Fair Trade as a Tool to Strengthen Community Democracy and Autonomy

Co-operative Press

Co-operative Press is an independent news organization, publisher, and co-operative society. Their mission is to discuss the global co-operative movement using journalistic objectivism, encouraging debate among readers.

W here Fairtrade-certified producers enjoy higher prices than non-certified farmers, it can be hard to isolate the factors behind this differential.

Access to Fairtrade Markets

A key part of Fairtrade is that a minimum price is paid to certified producers for certified products. Minimum prices are set and adjusted periodically for specific regions, based on a methodology estimating the average cost of sustainable production. They are designed as a safety net for producers when market prices are low.

Fairtrade certification can provide important forms of price security during periods of market crisis, such as the coffee crisis of 2000-2004, through the Fairtrade Minimum Price mechanism.

But in cases where Fairtrade-certified producers enjoy higher prices than non-certified farmers, it can be difficult to isolate the factors behind this differential, which may include differences in quality, value added by the organisation, and the bargaining power of the producer organisation. In other words, market context may determine the price differentials earned by Fairtrade producers as well as the Fairtrade certification per se. The effects of price differentials (and indeed the Fairtrade Premiums, discussed later) depend on the extent of access to Fairtrade markets: the proportion of crop sold through Fairtrade channels.

"How Much Difference Does Fairtrade Make—and How Can We Measure It?"
Co-operative Press Ltd (www.thenews.coop), February 2, 2018. Reprinted by permission.

The market for Fairtrade—still primarily in Europe, North America and Australia/New Zealand—fluctuates and grows. Fairtrade makes efforts to increase market demand; to support and advise producers in relation to market potential; and to link interested buyers with certified producers.

However, in most cases—and particularly with coffee—certified supply outstrips demand, leading to limitations on access to Fairtrade markets, with various unintended consequences in terms of competition between certified producers. Balancing supply with demand is one of the challenges of the movement, particularly given the time-lag in preparing producer organisations for certification.

Farming Performance and the Environment

There has been limited emphasis on farming performance and improvement in crop yields within Fairtrade certification, though it has been growing over time.

Other certification systems, such as Good Agricultural Practice (GAP) and UTZ Certified, have emphasised increased yields, product quality and attributes as a way to improve producers' incomes.

Fairtrade has focused more on regulating prices, trading relationships, strengthening organisations and governance. Its certification requirements have not focused on "good agricultural practice" or specific measures to increase yields or quality.

Indeed, a high proportion of Fairtrade-certified producers are also certified organic, which is also likely to influence yields. Evidence has been found of Fairtrade-certified farmers achieving higher yields than non-certified farmers, though the reasons for this were usually hard to disaggregate.

It may be partly due to the strengthening of organisational structures and services that result from Fairtrade certification, or from extension programmes that may be associated with it. It may also be due to the prior selection of farmers for certification who were already achieving higher yields. In some cases, Fairtrade buyers or other intermediaries may add or incentivise quality requirements when selecting farmers.

Comparative studies have also shown that other certification schemes which focus primarily on "good agricultural practice" are more closely correlated with higher yield production, though these studies face the same potential problem of selection bias. Fairtrade objectives are much clearer for environmental protection. Achievement of defined standards on such issues as management of water and soil use, pest control and use of pesticides, fertiliser application and biodiversity conservation are included as Fairtrade Standards for both small producer organisations and plantations.

Research shows positive impacts of certification and environment-related standards on farming practices in small producer organisations and plantations. But given the prevalence of joint Fairtrade-Organic certification, this may be due, in part, to the organic certification process. Other research found that these positive effects may result from the strength of co-operative organisation, or from agroecological approaches promoted by other organisations, rather than from Fairtrade certification per se.

Investment of the Fairtrade Premium

The Fairtrade Premium is set periodically for each certified commodity and each region. This is usually a fixed payment per unit of weight, or as a percentage of the commercial price paid, for commodities where no minimum price is set. This is one of the most visible pathways for Fairtrade impact, and is more easily differentiated than the wider impacts of minimum prices or the application of Fairtrade Standards.

Many qualitative studies discuss three types of benefit from the Fairtrade Premium: community benefits, such as local infrastructure, health and education; benefits focused on certified producers or plantation workers and their families, such as education scholarships, production-related services including loans; and support for operations of producer organisations, such as buildings and processing facilities. Similar benefits were described for workers on certified plantations.

In a study of the Ghanaian Fairtrade-certified cocoa producers' organisation, Kuapa Kokoo, Nelson et al. (2013) reported that 49.84% of the Fairtrade Premium was spent on incentives and social projects, followed by 19.2% on the organisation's own internal control system. The Kuapa Kokoo website lists the social projects funded by the Fairtrade Premium: 348 bore holes, eight schools, six toilet blocks, 51 corn mills and one cassava flakes processor. Certified farmers were largely unaware of these and did not distinguish between investments from the Fairtrade Premium or from the organisation's other sources.

Several authors quoted cases of certified farmers complaining about expenditure of the Fairtrade Premium on community projects that included benefits for non-certified farmers who had not contributed, and some expressed a preference that individual farmers should earn directly the Fairtrade Premium paid on the crop sold through Fairtrade channels.

In some cases, the management of the Fairtrade Premium was found ineffective, reducing impacts. In their study of six coffee co-ops within the Oromia Coffee Co-operative Union in Ethiopia, Jena et al. (2012) found difficulties resulting from this federated structure. As the Fairtrade specialist from the union has mentioned, "until the certified co-operatives or farmers write a project proposal and submit it to the union, the [Fairtrade] Premium is kept at the union." So the certified co-ops and producers did not receive as much of the social premium as they should.

Strength and Democracy

Fairtrade stipulates that small farmers cannot be certified as individuals but must form a functioning and formally constituted organisation. Fairtrade certification for small producer organisations requires a variety of standards to be met in terms of structure, organisation and democratic procedures.

This is an important objective of Fairtrade as well as a prerequisite for meeting and verifying other standards required for certification.

The BSD Consulting report on the impact of Fairtrade orange juice production in Brazil (BSD, 2014), linked support for the development of strong co-op structures through Fairtrade certification with the very survival of smallholder orange cultivation for the juice industry in the face of competition from large-scale plantations.

"We can state that the existence and survival of the co-operatives as such can be seen as a major impact of Fairtrade. In the orange market, survival of small producers is intrinsically linked to their capacity to build co-operatives and join their forces. Under the current circumstances (difficulty in selling to industries and exposure to low prices, lack of own processing assets), the business continuation of single small orange producers is at risk … The only way out is the creation of strong associations between smallholders in order to join the production and sales forces."

Some studies have also tried to collect evidence from members of certified producer organisations to shed light on organisational strength and democracy. Such evidence is case-specific and the indicators used can only act as proxy indicators of actual organisational strength and weakness. Ruben and Zuniga (2011), in their study of certified and non-certified coffee producers in northern Nicaragua, found that members of Fairtrade co-ops identified strongly with them and were satisfied with their membership: "In institutional aspects, [Fairtrade] performs better compared to independent producers in terms of organisational support provided by the co-operative and some attitudinal effects.

"Identification and satisfaction with the co-operative organisation are generally strong amongst [Fairtrade] members (compared to individual and Café Practices producers), but co-operative services of farmers delivering under the Rainforest Alliance label are even more appreciated."

Other studies highlighted the potential threat to co-operative trust and unity from co-operative leadership control of resources, such as the Fairtrade Premium. One research paper tried to test whether the experience of membership of strong and well-managed certified producer organisations helped to develop higher levels of trust and social capital more widely within the membership and community, but did not find positive evidence.

Decent Work Conditions

Fairtrade Standards for hired labour cover a wide range of terms and conditions, including: freedom from discrimination; freedom from forced and compulsory labour; prevention of child labour for children under 15; freedom of association and collective bargaining. They include provisions on the conditions of employment, including wages.

Evidence on the impact of Fairtrade certification on labour standards and work conditions is positive. Raynolds (2012 and 2014) conducted a study of four Fairtrade-certified flower farms in Ecuador. This industry has been well known for abuse of workers' rights. Companies have avoided labour protection legislation by hiring through intermediaries and firing workers after three-month probation periods. Unpaid overtime is common. Sexual harassment and child labour is widely reported.

Raynolds found the impact of certification in the industry was positive in terms of health and safety and created some improvement in labour conditions. Minimum wage and child labour requirements mirrored national law but better standards were mandated in some areas, including the prevention of abusive management and discriminatory practices and more generous overtime and annual leave.

But a number of authors have examined the impact of Fairtrade on conditions of workers in certified small producer organisations and found limited impact on wages or working conditions. The Valkila and Nygren (2010) study on coffee production in Nicaragua concluded that Fairtrade certification had very limited impact on wages or working conditions.

Wages for coffee labourers on Fairtrade-certified farms ranged from US$1.5 to US$2.1 per day on farms that also provided meals, and US$1.8 to US$2.5 on those that did not. Some farmers said they had increased wages to meet national minimum wage standards but none mentioned doing so to meet Fairtrade Standards. Given widespread underemployment, most farmers said workers were already fortunate to be receiving the minimum wage, and therefore did not provide other benefits such as holidays or sick leave. Children were frequently seen working on small certified family farms but this was family rather than contracted labour and subject to different controls.

Income, Wellbeing and Resilience

Arguably the central concern of most of the evaluations and assessments is Fairtrade's contribution to household income, wellbeing and resilience. Many of the mechanisms of Fairtrade—such as the Fairtrade Minimum Price, the Fairtrade Premium, quality and yield improvements, standards on decent work—contribute to this.

Examples of positive impacts on household income were included by Chiputwa et al. (2015) in their study of the differential effects of Fairtrade, organic and UTZ certification on coffee farmers in central Uganda. The team found that income benefits of certification were significant and driven by Fairtrade certification. "Looking at the first comparison between certified and non-certified farmers, we find that certification increases consumption expenditure by UGX 369-479 per capita per day (PPP $0.5-$0.63).

"This effect is significant and implies an increase in living standard by 12-15% when compared to mean expenditure of non-certified households. However, the effects on household poverty are not statistically significant.

"Disaggregating by certification scheme, we find that the positive impact on household expenditure is entirely driven by

Fairtrade certification. Participation in Fairtrade increases per capita expenditure by 27-33%, while the effects of UTZ and organic are both insignificant.

"Likewise we find significant poverty-reducing effects for Fairtrade, but not for UTZ and Organic. Participation in Fairtrade reduces the poverty headcount index by 0.13 to 0.15, implying a 50% reduction of the poverty rate observed among non-certified households."

Other surveys found evidence of income benefits from Fairtrade certification, but only for certain categories of farmer. Dragusanu and Nunn (2014) used data on coffee production in Costa Rica from Instituto del Café de Costa Rica (ICAFE) as well as Fairtrade data from certified co-operatives (2003-2010). "We find that Fairtrade certification does increase incomes, but only for skilled coffee growers and farm owners. There is no evidence that many workers, including unskilled seasonal coffee pickers, benefit from certification."

Quantitative evidence on income effects is also mixed. A number of studies have shown no impacts, or very limited impacts of Fairtrade certification on smallholder incomes. Given the previous discussion of some of the Fairtrade impact mechanisms, this is not surprising. For example, minimum prices only have direct impact when market prices are low. And income effects also depend on the proportion of output sold through Fairtrade channels. Fairtrade Standards do not explicitly address the issue of yields and quality, which may be more dependent on contextual factors.

Gender Equality

In terms of concrete provisions on gender, Fairtrade Standards for small producer organisations are relatively limited. They include clear provisions against discrimination on a number of grounds, including gender and standards banning forced labour, with specific mention of human trafficking for labour or sexual exploitation. Standards also require adherence to national law on maternity leave.

While certified organisations need to adhere to guidelines on inclusion, transparency and democracy in decision-making, these do not cover specific requirements in terms of gender equality.

Similarly, in hired labour situations, Fairtrade does not mandate women's participation as worker representatives on Fairtrade Premium Committees, stating only that composition should reflect the membership of the workforce, including in terms of gender. In relation to capacity-building, the standards require companies to "give special attention to the empowerment of women by means of adequate training, capacity-building, guidance, encouragement and assistance as necessary."

Evidence of Fairtrade impacts tend to derive more from qualitative studies, and to focus on women's voices and roles in governance structures rather than on differential economic impacts on women.

Some studies have found direct benefits to women producers in terms of increased recognition of land ownership, membership of associations and access to better prices.

Lyon et al. (2010) carried out a study of coffee producer organisations in Mexico and Guatemala, in the context of the general feminisation of labour in Meso-America due to high rates of male out-migration. The study used data from the State Coordinator of Oaxacan Coffee Producers. The authors found that women were increasingly involved in coffee cultivation, particularly in picking, washing, drying and selection, though usually at lower wages than men. The proportion of work done by women also depended on the levels of mechanisation in different co-operatives, as well as variations in local practices.

Nelson and Smith (2011) in their survey of Fairtrade cotton production in Mali, Senegal and Cameroon, concluded that "improvements in women's representation and participation in Producer Organisations were found in all four case studies, although there is concern that women may still feel obliged to vote as their spouse does and board representation is sometimes only symbolic. Gendered social norms and the gender division of labour still limit women's participation and ability to benefit from Fairtrade."

In their study of coffee certification on smallholder farmers in Kenya, Uganda and Ethiopia, the Centre for International Development Issues Nijmegen CIDIN (2014) found that: "Certification influences decision-making procedures in the co-operative domain but women's bargaining position in the private domain remains largely unaffected, unless women are accepted as full members of the co-operative and are included in the board." However, "women are a very small minority in the co-operatives and among coffee farmers and play a limited role in the governance structures."

Much of the evidence suggests that improvements in the voice and role of women within producer organisations and hired labour situations resulting from adherence to Fairtrade Standards may be more formalistic in nature, and that such requirements may struggle to impact on actual gender norms and power relationships.

Existing gender norms in the communities and cultures in which Fairtrade operates also has an important role in determining its impact.

Fair Trade Reduces Child Labor and Exploitation

Fair Trade Australia New Zealand

Fair Trade Australia New Zealand is a branch of the Global Fair Trade network that promotes fair trade certified products and raises awareness for the benefits fair trade can bring to communities.

More than 151 million children, some as young as five, are engaged in harmful child labour instead of getting an education or playing. That's 151 million reasons to stop the practice.

Do you know who picked the coffee beans that went into your flat white this morning? What about the cotton in the shirt you're wearing? Here's an even tougher question: Do you know the age of the person harvesting the cocoa beans that went into your afternoon chocolate pick-me-up?

Around the world there are an estimated 151 million victims of child labour, aged 5-17, and the majority of them work in agriculture, including cocoa, coffee and cotton plantations. Half those children are under the age of 11, and almost 73 million of them work in hazardous conditions.

When children as young as five are in child labour, it affects everything else in their life, from their development to their education. And when children don't have access to an education, they lose out on the chance at a better future. That's why Fairtrade, and many other members of the global community, are working hard to eradicate this injustice.

But Lots of Children Aged Under 17 Have Part-Time Jobs, Right?

Confronting child labour is a challenging issue. In countries such as Australia and New Zealand the image of a child working is someone with a newspaper round before school, a teenager behind

"Fairtrade And Child Labour," Fairtrade Australia New Zealand. Reprinted by permission.

the counter of a fast food restaurant or possibly someone helping their mum or dad do jobs on the family farm before they get stuck into their homework. In Australia, for example, children can generally work from the age of 15 (without a special permit or under specific exceptions, and it varies by state), and getting a part-time job is usually encouraged—especially by parents! But in both countries those jobs come with controls about what children can and can't do, the hours they can work and whether it can interfere with their schooling. There is also support in place for employees—children or otherwise—who aren't being paid properly. Stringent safety laws exist to protect workers on the job, and children who are employed are not allowed to do dangerous work.

There's a huge difference between children in age-appropriate controlled employment that helps them develop skills and self-esteem, and the damaging, brutal reality faced by child labourers. The experiences are so different that the International Labour Organizaton even counts the 66 million children in employment separately to the child labour category.

If It's Not a Teenager Asking People If They'd Like Fries, Who Are Child Labourers and What Sort of Work Do They Do?

Child labour is predominantly used in agriculture, in fact that's where 71 percent of child labour—or 108 million children—is found. Just under 12 percent is found in industrial settings such as factories, and 17 percent provide services, such as cleaning or domestic help. The problem is that this is the child labour we know about. Although 58 million child labourers are boys and 42 million girls, girls are more likely at every age group to spend more hours a week in domestic labour, and they are also more likely to work both domestically and in another job.

It's incredibly difficult to get numbers of domestic labourers or children in sex work because they're hidden from the public eye. These roles are also more likely to be filled by girls, potentially in countries where girls are less visible anyway or seen as having fewer rights than boys or men. Girls may also not be valued as highly by their communities or families, so fewer concerns are raised about their well-being or whether their educational needs are being met.

The 38 million children aged between 15 and 17 years are also included in the figures as child labourers, not because they are too young to work, but because the work they are doing is too dangerous. Young workers have up to a 40 percent higher rate of non-fatal occupational injuries than workers over the age of 25.

How Bad Are the Worst Forms of Child Labour?

The worst forms of child labour can involve the sale or trafficking of children, debt bondage, forced or compulsory labour—including into armed forces as child soldiers, or into prostitution—using a child for the production or trafficking of drugs or any other work with a significant chance of harming a child, whether physically or psychologically.

Hazardous work is also no job for children, whether underground, under water, at dangerous heights or in confined spaces; with dangerous machinery, equipment and tools, or moving heavy loads; or where children are exposed to hazardous substances or processes, toxins or even high temperatures or noise levels.

But Can't Families Stop Their Children Working?

No parent would choose to see their child sacrificing the most basic education for work, or working in slave-like conditions, but poverty removes choices very fast. Part of the complexity of child labour is that more than two-thirds of it happens on family farms or in a family context, and families living in poverty need to have working children to survive. It's no surprise that in low-income (<\$US1,045 GNI per capita) countries one in five children work—but the problem is not limited to those places, with another 84 million children from middle-income (\$US1,046-\$US12,735) countries also in child labour. In upper-income (>\$US12,736) countries the number plummets to one in 100 (although that's still unacceptable).

There's also a strong causal link between conflict, natural disasters and displacement, and child labour, and according to UNICEF, 535 million children—or a quarter of children worldwide—live in countries affected by conflict or disaster. Children also make up more than half the 65 million people who have been displaced by war. Unrest, disasters and displacement make children vulnerable to a range of exploitation, not just labour. Sometimes children find themselves on their own, or even if they are still with family members or carers the household may have lost its income, home or possessions, and support networks. Even short-term crises that are soon resolved can force children out of school just for long enough to stop them going back.

Is There Any Good News?

Yes! Eradicating child labour was one of the Millennium Development Goals (MDGs) and the combined efforts of the global community made a lot of progress. There were about 94 million fewer children in child labour in 2016 than there were in 2000. And the number of children doing hazardous work has fallen by more than half, from 170 million to 72.5 million. The Sustainable Development Goals, announced in 2015 to replace the MDGs, include the ambitious commitment to end child labour in all its forms by 2025. But that won't happen through policy-making alone, every single person is going to have to commit to a world without child labour to bring about SDG target 8.7 by demanding transparent supply chains and corporate responsibility for the production of their goods.

What Is Fairtrade Doing to Help End Child Labour?

Tackling child labour is one of the core principles of Fairtrade, and it's an issue that has to be addressed by any producer organization and its members before they can become Fairtrade certified.

Small producer organizations and their members must:

- Not employ children under the age of 15 or under the age of local laws, whichever is higher;
- Make all efforts to work out the ages of children working with their parents, and that those children are only working after school or during holidays, are not doing heavy or dangerous labour, are well supervised, and are not working long hours;
- Encourage children to attend school or work with local authorities to build a school or provide transport to a school if one isn't available in the area;
- Ensure children under the age of 18 do not do dangerous work, or work that is likely to affect their health, safety or school attendance;
- Support any former child labourers to make sure they are not vulnerable to worse forms of labour or exploitation if they can no longer be employed due to Fairtrade requirements.

Making sure farmers and producers receive a fair price for their produce and their labour is one of the first steps to helping alleviate poverty and the need for child labour. When a family becomes financially stable it is better placed to ensure children attend school and can have bright futures of their own. Another way Fairtrade can help is through the Fairtrade Premium—an additional amount that is paid to cooperatives on top of the Fairtrade Minimum Price, that cooperatives can spend as they choose to benefit their members or the community. In some places the Premium has been used as a source of funding for schools or school transport.

You Said Everyone Needs to Commit to Make the End of Child Labour a Reality, But What Can I Do?

You can use your purchasing power to help eradicate child labour by choosing to buy products—such as coffee, chocolate and tea—with the Fairtrade Mark. Look for the Fairtrade logo when you shop to make sure you are supporting producers and supply chains that have rejected child labour, and help us work towards a child-labour free world by 2025.

Producers Weigh In on the Benefits They Received Through Fair Trade

Rachel Dixon

Rachel Dixon is a journalist who works on travel and features at the Guardian.

Does buying Fairtrade products really make a difference to people's lives? Rachel Dixon talks to three producers and finds out how their communities have been transformed.

Gerardo Arias Camacho, Coffee Producer, Costa Rica

Gerardo is a coffee farmer in Llano Bonito, San José, Costa Rica. He is a board member on his village cooperative, which is a member of the Fairtrade consortium COOCAFE. He is married with three children.

In the 1980s, the price of coffee fell so low that it didn't cover the cost of production. Many farmers abandoned their land and went to the cities to find work. Some even left the country. In the mid-90s, I decided to go to America to make money and support my family. After eight years, I had earned enough to buy the family farm so that my parents could retire. But coffee prices were still so low that I was forced to go back to the States for another two years.

The coffee market was so unstable. We did not have a local school, good roads or bridges. Now that our consortium is Fairtrade-certified, prices are stable and we receive a guaranteed premium. We spend the money on education, environmental protection, roads and bridges, and improving the old processing plant. We have sponsored a scholarship programme so that our kids can stay in school.

"'Teach Us How to Fish—Do Not Just Give Us the Fish,'" by Rachel Dixon, Guardian News and Media Limited, March 12, 2008. Reprinted by permission.

I believe that my cooperative would be out of business if it wasn't for Fairtrade. Free trade is not responsible trade. When prices go down, farmers produce more and prices drop further. Fairtrade is the way trade should be: fair, responsible and sustainable.

My oldest son is in college, my ten-year-old has already had as much education as me, and my little princess is in her second year at school. With the help of Fairtrade, they might all be able to go to university and get a degree. They won't have to jump the border from Mexico to America, leaving their country for ten years, like me. They can decide what they want in life. I tell them: "You have two choices. You can be a coffee grower or you can be something else. But learn how to be a coffee grower first, like your father and your grandfather." Since Fairtrade, our farms have become more environmentally friendly. Our coffee is now produced in a sustainable way. We have planted trees and reduced the use of pesticides by 80% in 10 years. We used to cut 20 hectares (50 acres) of forest down every year to fuel the ovens at our processing plant. Now we have a new oven which is fuelled by waste products, including coffee skins and the skins of macadamia nuts that we buy from farmers on the other side of Costa Rica. It is a win-win business.

Fairtrade is not a closed system, it is open to everyone. But we need more and more people to buy Fairtrade so that the market grows and other farmers can become certified. Fairtrade can be a tool to help farmers who are not certified. We educate the producers around us about market prices so that buyers have to offer them a competitive rate. It also benefits the wider community. When there was a hurricane, the new road became blocked and the bridge came down. We could afford to open the road and fix the bridge.

When you are shopping, look for the Fairtrade label—you can be sure that the money is going straight to the producers. It will help us, but it will also help people around the world, because the benefits of protecting the environment are for everyone. It is a matter of helping each other.

As a Fairtrade farmer, I finally feel competitive—I feel that I have a tool in my hand. It has given me knowledge, so that I am more able to defend myself and my people. I feel there is a future in front of us, because we can stay in our own country and make a living growing coffee.

Fairtrade is not charity. Just by going shopping, you can make a difference.

Julius Ethang'atha, Tea Producer, Kenya

Julius is a retired tea producer from Michimikuru, Kenya. He helped to introduce Fairtrade tea production to Kenya five years ago, while working for the Kenya Tea Development Agency (KTDA).

You can't keep all your eggs in the same basket, so we try many things in Kenya. I tried tea. When I was working for the KTDA, buyers asked for Fairtrade. It wasn't easy to become certified, but I saw it was the best way out for our people.

There was a huge impact on the first communities to work with Fairtrade. They were poor communities; they did not have water, dispensaries or schools close to them. The money they got from tea was used for food and clothes, but now they also get a premium that they can use to improve their social living. So far they have set up impressive schools and daycare centres, dispensaries, maternity units, water systems, bridges and roads.

I think criticism of Fairtrade is ridiculous. Yes, Fairtrade only accounts for a small share of the cake, but it is growing. Saying "Do not buy Fairtrade, because it doesn't help non-Fairtrade producers" is like saying "Do not eat, because others are hungry."

Africa does not need aid; we need to participate in a fairer trading system. Teach us how to fish—do not just give us the fish. You see, the farmer receives just 5% of the wealth in tea. When the consumer pays more for Fairtrade tea, this extra money goes to the farmer and improves lives. But if the whole value chain was made fairer, Africa would be lifted out of poverty.

Fairtrade is the right way to shop. It puts a smile on the faces of children in Africa, and it makes their lives bearable.

Makandianfing Keita, Cotton Farmer, Mali

Makandianfing is a cotton farmer in Dougourakoroni village, Mali, west Africa. The village cotton farmers are members of the UC-CPC de Djidian cooperative, which has been Fairtrade-certified since 2005. Makandianfing married last year.

Cotton prices were going down and down until they were below the cost of production. People were demotivated and it was very depressing. But now, we can make a sustainable living. My family can eat and we have better health.

In the past, children had to walk 10km to go to school, so really it was impossible. We have now been able to build a school. At first it had two classrooms. When we had more money and wanted to expand, we challenged the government to match our investment. Now there are five classrooms in total, and every child in the village can go to school.

Pregnant women had no access to healthcare. Many died in childbirth and there were high rates of infant mortality. Now we have built a maternity centre. We have also built a food storage facility so that we can have a year-round food supply, and we have installed a pump for drinking water. We have built a new road, enabling us to travel further than 5km outside of the village without difficulty.

Fairtrade standards called for better agricultural practices. Before, empty pesticide containers would be used as water carriers. In some cases this led to death. Now, we dispose of waste properly. We don't burn bushes any more, we prevent soil erosion and we have effective irrigation.

Fairtrade has really changed the life of my community. I feel as though I have a future, which I didn't before. My wife is pregnant with our first child—this is how optimistic we are!

I encourage everyone to buy more Fairtrade products if they want to make an impact on millions of lives.

Fair Trade Reduces Human Trafficking and Protects Children

Hannah Gould

Hannah Gould works for UNICEF USA's End Trafficking Campaign. Her writing has been featured in publications around the world. She is also a member of the New York State Anti-Trafficking Coalition.

I magine you are a child.

You are 12 years old and you have a mother, a father, and four younger siblings. Your family was forced to leave your home after extreme violence destroyed surrounding areas, including where your father went to work and where you and your siblings attended school. Now you live in a camp made of tents and temporary shelters and your parents are struggling to provide enough food for you and your family.

One day, a man stops you on the street and asks if you'd like a job. He needs a dishwasher for his restaurant in the city, only a day's journey away, and promises you food, a place to stay, and enough money to send back to your parents. He guarantees he'll handle all of the paperwork and transportation.

You think of your mother and father and how hard they are working. You think of your younger brothers and sisters and how they haven't had the energy to play since you've moved—their voices asking you "Do you think we'll have food tomorrow?"

So you run home and share the offer with your parents. They are hesitant to let you go away with this stranger—but the opportunity to have extra money and one less mouth to feed may be the blessing they've been waiting for.

When you arrive at the restaurant, you're told you must work to pay off the costs of your transportation, recruitment, and paperwork. In addition, every time you are late or you make a mistake, the amount you owe is doubled. You sleep on the floor

"How Fairtrade Helps End Trafficking," by Hannah Gould, Fairtrade America, August 2, 2016. Reprinted by permission.

in the storage closet, you work from sunrise until midnight, and you are not allowed to go outside or use the phone.

After a few months go by and you still owe more money than you've made, you consider running away and going back to your family. But your boss tells you he has police watching the restaurant, looking to make sure you don't leave and, if you do, they'll arrest you and you'll never see your family again. So you are trapped in a never-ending cycle of debt, in a city you can't navigate, under constant fear, with no way to communicate with your family or ask for help.

This is how millions of children are exploited in today's modern world. This is human trafficking.

Human trafficking, often compared to modern-day slavery, systematically exploits men, women, and children by forcing them to work unbearably long hours, under inhumane conditions, for little to no pay. It exists across continents and is facilitated through a variety of venues, but ultimately—human trafficking is an industry that profits from the exploitation of the world's most vulnerable.

The International Labor Organization (ILO) estimates that 20.9 million people are victims of forced labor and human trafficking and 5.5 million of those are children.

Children are trafficked into situations of debt bondage in the labor sector. Children can also be trafficked into agriculture, construction, mining, retail, forced child begging, and domestic servitude (to name a few) or trafficked into the commercial sex trade to work in strip clubs, prostitution or pornography, or in illicit massage parlors.

Legally defined in 2000, child trafficking is the "recruitment, transportation, transfer, harboring or receipt of children for the purpose of exploitation." It is closely related to, but distinct from child labor, which is defined as "work that harms the mental, physical, emotional well-being of child and/or interferes with his/her right to education and safety." Child trafficking and child labor are intertwined. Both involve exploitation and stem from similar root causes such as extreme poverty, lack of access to education and job opportunities, mass displacement, harmful social norms, and mass conflict. You cannot end child trafficking without addressing child labor, and vice versa.

How Fairtrade Can Help

So how does Fairtrade help reduce child trafficking? Below are six ways Fairtrade works to protect children from exploitation:

Small-scale farmers and workers who receive fairer pay can better provide for their families, send their children to school, and avoid the intergenerational cycles of poverty that push children into situations of exploitation and trafficking.

The Fairtrade Premium, paid in addition to the purchase price of products at the farmer level, help producers to bolster their communities against poverty. Premiums are invested into education, healthcare, business development and other important services that can allow families and children to have expanded access to important programs and services.

Fairtrade's internationally-agreed Fairtrade Standards help farmers and workers tackle poverty on their own terms in some of the poorest countries in the world. The standards encourage long-term relationships and fairer contracts for farmers, and require employers to protect the basic rights of the people they employ by upholding decent working conditions, allowing collective bargaining and freedom of association, paying wages that move towards country-specific living wage benchmarks, preventing discrimination. The Fairtrade Standards also prohibit child labor.

Qualified auditors inspect Fairtrade producers on a regular basis and pay special attention to certain areas and products where child labor is a risk. In addition, depending on the findings, Fairtrade suspends or de-certifies the producer organization where these worst forms of labor (e.g. child trafficking) are found until protective and corrective measures are put in place.

If child labor is detected, Fairtrade takes immediate action to address it and to protect the children involved in accordance with Fairtrade's Child Labor and Forced Labor Guidelines. Fairtrade producer organizations must build partnerships with local civil society organizations and child rights organizations to remediate situations of abuse or exploitation and ensure children do not become revictimized.

Fairtrade works with communities to set up Youth Inclusive Community Based Monitoring and Remediation (YICBMR) programs to help people take charge of issues around child labor. Children, young people and adults are at the heart of the program and identify potential and/or actual risks of children's wellbeing and make recommendations on how to respond. The YICBMR program has been piloted in 12 countries over the last three years.

How You Can Help

These are only six examples of the many ways Fairtrade works to end human trafficking. But the greatest way Fairtrade can make an impact is through consumers like you. Consumers yield a unique power to shape the way farmers and workers are treated and reduce exploitation around the world. Like any industry, human trafficking operates out of the basic principles of supply and demand. So when consumers demand ethically-made products, free of exploitation and child labor, companies will listen. Fairtrade offers consumers a simple way to help reduce poverty, protect children, and prevent trafficking. If you'd like to learn more about human trafficking and take action to protect children, follow these steps below:

- Start a Fair Trade Campaign with your school, university, congregation or community! Download resources on fairtrade products, access social media materials and learn more about what it means to start a campaign at fairtradecampaigns.com.
- Go to SlaveryFootprint.org to learn your connection to modern-day slavery and write to your favorite brands to ask them for stronger policies against child and forced labor!
- Discover where to buy fairtrade products online and in your local community!
- Host a fair trade lunch, dinner, or coffee hour to raise awareness about human trafficking. Educate and mobilize your own communities on the connection between labor trafficking and fair trade.

Fair Trade's High Startup Fees Hurt Poor Countries

Addison Arnold

Addison Arnold is a business analyst at USAA. She was an intern for the Heritage Foundation and participated in their Young Leaders Program.

Many Americans are seeking out so-called fair trade products in their local markets. They are willing to pay higher prices in hopes of improving incomes and working conditions for people in developing countries. But, in their paper "Fair Trade and Free Entry: Can a Disequilibrium Market Serve as a Development Tool?," economists Alain de Janvry, Craig McIntosh and Elisabeth Sadoulet uncover a startling truth—fair trade is actually quite unfair.

The term "fair trade" can have different meanings. In this case, it refers to products from industries that comply with fair trade organization standards in order to be designated a fair trade employer.

These employers provide higher wages and benefits to their workers, and hope—because of "fair trade" branding—to command a higher price in the global market. This idea may seem enticing, but it doesn't stand up to scrutiny. Fair trade practices are economically inefficient in the long run.

For example, Janvry's, McIntosh's and Sadoulets' research shows what actually happens in the fair trade coffee market.

In the most common fair trade scenario, coffee growers pay additional fees and adhere to regulations in order to sell coffee at a guaranteed minimum price, or price floor. However, such price differentials don't last. The study found that, typically, the market price adjusts, ending up being just as high as the fair trade price

"No Fair! How 'Fair Trade' Hurts Poor Countries," by Addison Arnold, The Heritage Foundation, August 4, 2015. Reprinted by permission.

floor, so employers essentially incurred costs to be labeled "fair trade" for no additional profit.

In other cases, fair trade companies are able to sell their coffee at a higher price than the market and make higher profits for a time; in the long run, however, Janvry's, McIntosh's and Sadoulets' study reveals that, as more and more coffee companies enter the fair trade market, coffee prices return to an equilibrium.

Each scenario demonstrates that fair trade does not boost profits in the long run, because prices naturally adjust to the market clearing price.

What about those higher prices paid by well-meaning consumers? Surely that helps someone! It turns out that most of those profits accrue to retailers here, not the growers in developing countries.

Moreover, fair trade can actually harm workers in the poorest developing countries. In his online video, professor of economics Don Boudreaux explains that only companies in relatively rich developing countries, such as Costa Rica, can afford the start-up fees for fair trade. Meanwhile, companies in extremely poor countries, such as Ethiopia, are not able to join fair trade markets. Therefore, fair trade singles out a few developing countries for short-term success while leaving the poorest countries by the wayside. Is that fair?

Basic economic principles indicate that fair trade does not help workers in the way that proponents had hoped. Even so, the question remains: What is the best way to improve wages in developing countries? The answer is: competition. Instead of isolating a few winners for short-term "fair" benefits, competition within a free market gives workers in all nations a shot to make a living wage. In the end, free trade is the fairest trade of all.

Fair Trade Is a Contributor to Poverty

Christopher Cramer

Christopher Cramer is a professor of the political economy of development at SOAS, University of London. He is also a member of the Centre of African Studies and the Centre on Conflict, Rights, and Justice.

The findings of our research may be disturbing for Fairtrade officials and for ordinary people who hope to make a difference to the plight of poor rural people in developing countries through informed choices about the products they buy.

But how well-informed are the choices that consumers make? Is Fairtrade fair for all involved in the production of tea, coffee and other commodities? The Fairtrade, Employment and Poverty Reduction in Ethiopia and Uganda project set out to improve our understanding of how global trade in agricultural commodities affects the lives of poor rural Africans, especially through wage employment.

Our research took four years and involved a great deal of fieldwork in Africa. We carried out detailed surveys, we collected oral histories, we talked to managers of co-operatives, to owners of flower companies, to traders and government officials, to auditors, to very young children working for wages instead of going to school, to people who had done fairly well out of Fairtrade, and to people who appeared not to have benefited.

It did not come as a huge surprise to us to learn from our data that people who depend for their survival on access to manual agricultural wage employment, often as seasonal or casual labour, are much poorer than others in the same area. Their diet is poorer. They own fewer assets—watches, pieces of furniture, mobile phones. And in the households where these people live, girls and women have less schooling.

"Harsh Truths Are Necessary if Fairtrade Is to Change the Lives of the Very Poor," by Christopher Cramer, Guardian News and Media Limited, May 24, 2014. Reprinted by permission.

We also knew that Fairtrade standards for tea and coffee have always been far more concerned with the incomes of producers than with wage workers' earnings. What did surprise us is how wages are typically lower, and on the whole conditions worse, for workers in areas with Fairtrade organisations than for those in other areas.

Careful statistical analysis allowed us to separate out the possible effects of other factors, such as the scale of production. Still, the differences were in most cases, and especially for wages, statistically significant. Explaining why it should be that workers in areas dominated by Fairtrade organisations are so often worse off than workers in other areas is a complex and challenging task. Our full report explores some possible reasons.

It was also surprising to learn that many people do not benefit from the "community" projects supported with funds generated by the "social premium" consumers pay for Fairtrade products. Researchers at Soas, University of London, formerly know as the School of Oriental and African Studies, found that many of the poorest are unable to use these facilities. In one Fairtrade tea co-operative the modern toilets funded with the premium were exclusively for the use of senior co-op managers.

One of our interviewees, James in Uganda, is desperately poor and lives with his elderly father in an inadequate shack very close to a tea factory supported by Fairtrade. Despite the fact that his father was once a worker at the tea factory, James is charged fees at the factory's Fairtrade health clinic. He cannot afford them and instead has to make his way on one leg to a government clinic more than 5km away to get free treatment.

At another Ugandan co-operative supported by Fairtrade, we spoke to poor children who had been turned away from the Fairtrade-supported school as they owed fees. In this case, the Fairtrade premium did not support the very poor but was used to build houses for the teachers.

What comes out of this research is that what we buy in supermarkets could make a difference to the lives of the poorest, those employed in producing the goods we buy. But it is difficult for shoppers to make informed choices.

Wages and working conditions vary significantly across employers. There are many off-the-peg but unconvincing reasons given for paying people shockingly little: it is what the price of coffee allows, you can't pay more when there is an excess supply of people wanting the jobs, and so on. But then it is surprising to find that there are employers who evidently can pay much more. This variation is what our research allows us to explore.

And in the process it raises questions for Fairtrade. If we are interested in what makes a difference to extremely poor people, it is important to compare areas with Fairtrade organisations not only with other smallholder producing areas, which we did, but also with areas where producers are much larger. If larger farmers can pay better and offer more days of work, this is surely an important thing to understand. It is not the "distorted comparison" that Fairtrade alleges.

We hope that our findings will help to inform consumers' choices and feed into Fairtrade's efforts to establish an auditing process that is more relevant to the lives of the poorest rural people. And we hope that they will commit to clearer information for consumers about who benefits from the social premium and how well rural wages and working conditions are monitored.

Fair Trade Fails Producers and Tricks Consumers

Bruce Wydick

Bruce Wydick is a professor of economics and international studies at the University of San Francisco. He specializes in economic development analysis and is the author of several academic publications on the impact of development programs.

I see you, smugly smiling over your morning cup of fair-trade coffee, gratified at the unimaginable impact your thoughtfully chosen beans must be bringing to poor coffee growers overseas.

Well, think again.

The academic evidence for any positive effect of fair-trade coffee on coffee growers is mixed at best. Several recent studies by researchers at Harvard, the University of Wisconsin, and the University of California indicate that fair-trade coffee has small to negligible effects on coffee growers, especially the poorest ones. The University of California researchers find that the lack of impact stems from the ill-conceived design of the fair-trade system. Indeed, a consensus among development economists indicates fair-trade coffee to be one of the least effective means for reducing poverty in developing countries.

Here's how the fair-trade system, overseen by the Fairtrade Labelling Organizations International (FLO) and its U.S. certification affiliate, Fair Trade USA, operates: Growers belonging to a selected group of overseas producer cooperatives are paid a minimum price of $1.40 per pound (in the case of Arabica beans) for all coffee that is able to be sold through fair-trade channels. This minimum price creates what economists call a "price floor" for fair-trade growers. If the market price rises higher than the price floor (as it has today, at nearly $2.00 per pound), then growers

"10 Reasons Fair-Trade Coffee Doesn't Work," by Bruce Wydick, January 28, 2016. Reprinted by permission.

just receive the market price, along with a premium of $0.20 that is sent back for investment in the producer cooperative and the local community. In order to receive this price, growers must pay to become certified, join a democratically managed cooperative, agree to standards for pesticide and chemical fertilizer use, and pay "fair wages" to coffee laborers.

All of this is well-intentioned and sounds wonderful. The problem is that is doesn't work well. The University of California study shows how the fair-trade system fails to account for basic economic laws that undercut its benefits to growers, among other fundamental flaws.

Here are 10 reasons that fair-trade coffee doesn't do the amount of good you would expect:

1. The flawed design of the system undermines its own benefits. Recent research by development economists Alain de Janvry and Betty Sadoulet at U.C. Berkeley and Craig McIntosh at U.C. San Diego shows that when the world price of coffee falls (and the advantages of selling through fair-trade channels increase), more borrowers choose to obtain fair-trade certification. But this reduces the fraction of coffee that their cooperatives can sell at the fair-trade price. What they found after examining 13 years of data from cooperatives in Guatemala is that, on average, the economic benefits of participating in the fair-trade system are offset by the price the growers have to pay for fair-trade certification. In other words, they found that the long-term benefit over time from fair trade to be essentially zero.

2. Fair trade attracts bad beans. Every crop contains some beans that are of higher quality than others. If the market price for the low-quality beans is below $1.40 and the market price of high-quality beans is above $1.40, then the fair-trade system incentivizes growers to dump their bad beans into fair-trade channels. As economists will lecture to you unceasingly, incentives matter. As the

bad beans are drawn into the fair-trade market (what economics calls "adverse selection"), potential buyers eschew buying the coffee for fear of being stuck with the low-quality beans. This phenomenon has limited the market for fair-trade coffee.

3. Fair trade imposes significant costs on impoverished growers. The University of California study estimates that fair-trade certification costs about $0.03 per pound. This doesn't sound like much, but in some years it is greater than any price benefit brought by the higher fair-trade price. Moreover, while restrictions on growing practices might seem to meet worthy environmental and social objectives, University of Wisconsin economist Brad Barham and colleagues find that costs to growers imposed by these restrictions on fertilizers and other inputs add to the production costs of impoverished growers, diminish yields, and mitigate the benefits of free trade. If coffee drinkers want to improve the environment, they should pay for it themselves, not impose added costs on impoverished coffee growers.

4. Fair trade doesn't help the poorest growers. In a recent study in Costa Rica, economists Raluca Dragusanu and Nathan Nunn at Harvard University found the modest benefits generated from fair trade to be concentrated among the most skilled coffee growers. They find no positive impact on coffee laborers, no positive impact on children's education, and negative impacts on the education of unskilled coffee workers' children. In contrast, the "impact reports" created by Fair Trade USA, which are available on their home page, are a series of documents that merely describe the nature and scope of the fair-trade programs for various commodities. These reports fail to demonstrate any positive impact of the program by any credible scientific standard of impact evaluation.

5. Relatively little fair-trade coffee originates from the poorest countries. The poorest coffee-growing countries are in Africa: Ethiopia, Kenya, and Tanzania. Fair-trade exports from these countries represent less than 10 percent of coffee marketed through fair trade, while the share of fair-trade coffee from middle-income countries such as Mexico, Brazil, and Colombia is many times higher. Effective poverty interventions should be targeted at most poor, not the medium-poor.

6. Purported benefits of the fair-trade system lack transparency. Although fair trade pays a $0.20 premium over the world coffee price to growers for "social and economic investments at the community and organizational level," how this money is actually spent in the home country is vague at best. In an article in the *Stanford Social Innovation Review*, California State University economist Colleen Haight finds that many of these funds are invested in coffee cooperatives' buildings and salaries, not in schools, which may explain why researchers fail to uncover positive impacts from fair trade on local education.

7. The fair-trade system is inefficient at transferring coffee consumers' goodwill to producers. In an experiment run by my graduate students in San Francisco (described in *The Taste of Many Mountains*), we found that the median coffee drinker is—amazingly—willing to pay a premium of 50 cents for a cup of fair-trade coffee. However, we find that even in the best-case scenario for fair trade, when world prices are at their lowest, the maximum amount a fair-trade grower from that same cup of coffee would receive is only *one third of a cent*.

8. Direct trade is probably more efficient and sustainable than fair trade. Under direct trade, a coffee buyer contracts directly with specific growers overseas to offer a higher coffee price, often in exchange for a higher-quality

product and a long-term relationship. Although direct trade is certainly not a panacea, more real value is created in the system, making it an arguably more efficient means of transmitting resources from coffee drinkers to coffee growers.

9. We should encourage less coffee production, not more. Efforts to help coffee growers by paying them more for their coffee all stimulate more coffee production, which is precisely the wrong way to help coffee growers. It is lower worldwide coffee production that brings the most benefit to each grower, by raising coffee prices. Thus the best approaches to helping coffee growers involve helping people move away from coffee production. Interventions in coffee communities like microfinance, cash grants to start new enterprises, and internationally sponsoring the children of coffee growers to help these children obtain more and better education help coffee growers worldwide because they reduce the world supply of coffee. This benefits everyone, because as coffee growers and their children move to other occupations, all producers in the world benefit from higher coffee prices. Artificially stimulating more coffee production keeps coffee growers poor.

10. Fair-trade coffee fails to address the root of poverty issues. Core poverty issues in developing countries suggest thoughtful, strategic interventions in areas such as health, education, infrastructure, entrepreneurial activity, and governance. If these core issues can be effectively addressed, a new array of occupational choices will open to the poor, allowing them to lift themselves out of rural poverty. Instead of providing credible evidence of impact in any of these key areas, fair-trade coffee incentivizes production of more coffee (see #9).

The most damaging aspect of the fair-trade coffee system may be that it misleads well-meaning coffee consumers into believing that by buying fair-trade coffee they are doing something meaningful and helpful for the poor, while the best evidence suggests that other types of programs are far more effective. And this tragically misdirects energy and attention away from approaches to fighting poverty that actually work quite well. Perhaps a main reason that fair-trade coffee continues to have credibility with many in the general population is the immense marketing campaign undertaken by Fair Trade USA, which continues to promote itself despite the self-neutralizing flaws in its poorly designed system.

In a recent magazine article, I surveyed 16 leading development economists to rate 10 common types of anti-poverty programs in terms of their effectiveness. Fair-trade coffee ranked second to last, ahead of only providing laptop computers to school children in poor countries (another intervention that has been rigorously studied and found to lack positive impacts on intended beneficiaries). Providing fresh water to rural villages finished first. Efforts to improve children's health through deworming campaigns and providing mosquito nets to mitigate malaria infection finished second and third. Sponsoring a child overseas was fourth. Providing clean-burning stoves to mitigate indoor air pollution and deforestation was fifth.

Let's focus on ways to help the poor that work—and leave behind the things that don't.

CHAPTER 4

Is Fair Trade Actually Fair?

The Two Sides of Fair Trade, Fair and Unfair

Sarah Morrison

Sarah Morrison is a writer for the Independent *and serves as their human rights correspondent.*

It is trade, of that there is no doubt. Some £1.3bn is spent on Fairtrade-badged goods in the UK. But nearly two decades after the launch of the scheme, the question that increasingly vexes consumers as they make their purchases is: is it really fair?

The UK is the world's biggest fair-trade market, and it continues to grow. The first three products to showcase the Fairtrade mark hit the shelves in this country 18 years ago. Now, days ahead of World Fair Trade Day, there are more than 4,500 products carrying the familiar logo in our shops.

The scheme was set up with the anything-but-simple mission of providing "better prices, decent working conditions, local sustainability, and fair terms of trade for farmers and workers in the developing world." Farmers who pay for certification are assured a minimum price—which can never fall below market level—and a premium to invest in their communities.

Sales of the fair-trade goods increased by 12 per cent in the UK between 2010 and 2011, and this year alone, Mars—the third biggest confectionery brand in the UK—will switch Maltesers to Fairtrade, representing more than a 10 per cent increase in total sales. Fairtrade has turned to certifying the gold industry in the past two years and is expecting to announce new standards for freshwater prawns this summer. Almost 40 per cent of all our bananas are now Fairtrade.

Despite becoming increasingly mainstream, the Fairtrade label has persistent critics. It is attacked by those on the left who say it has sold out and given in to the market. Pundits on the right

"Fairtrade: Is It Really Fair?" by Sarah Morrison, The *Independent*, May 6, 2012. Reprinted by permission.

argue that it distorts markets, exaggerates its claims, prices out the poorest farmers and perpetuates inefficient modes of production.

In the week when more than 70 countries will celebrate the notion of fair trade as a "tangible contribution to the fight against poverty," *The Independent on Sunday* looked behind the label to answer one pressing question: just how fair is fair trade?

"The Whole Town Depends on Mining—We Need Support"

Harbi Guerrero Morillo, 40, lives with his wife and one-year-old daughter in Colombia. For the past 14 years he has been running a mine, providing work for 30 workers. In his community, about 70 per cent of people are employed in mining-related activities and earn around £220 a month for their work. Almost 400 families benefit from the gold production. Mr Morillo's co-operative is in the process of becoming certified with Fairtrade and Fairmined, in order to become one of only a handful of mines to produce Fairtrade gold.

"We would take pride and show off our certified community because it would show that our gold is clean, exported and seen in a positive way. Sometimes the industry is frowned upon, and there are concerns that if mines don't comply with legislations, they will be closed down. Here, the whole town depends on mining— we need support. This certification could work as a road map for mining and it could open us up to how we could improve our communities and network with other miners. It is about legitimising my work—that is very important."

"The Fairtrade Price Does Not Change Throughout the Season"

Tomy Mathew, 50, is a spice and nut farmer from Kerala, India. He was one of the founding members of his local fair-trade alliance, which was established more than six years ago, after his region suffered an "agrarian crisis."

"Between 1992 and 2006, there was a terrible economic crisis for agriculture in Kerala. All the prices fell and this made us look for markets that offered fair deals to farmers. This year, the market price for cashews was about 62 rupees per kilo (71p). The fair-trade price came in at 75 rupees per kilo (86p). It's not the difference between the market and fair-trade prices that makes the most difference; it is the fact that the fair-trade price does not change throughout the season. It costs us $3,000 a year to get certified, but in the first year, we received a 75 per cent subsidy. It might be difficult to pay, but I wouldn't want them to lower the price—it ensures the credibility of the system."

"Fairtrade Is the Way Forward— We Can Make a Living"

Moses Rene, 34, is a banana farmer who lives with his wife, Robertina, in St Lucia. He works on their farm eight hours a day, six days a week, and is involved in his local Fairtrade farmers' group, a part of the Windward Islands Farmers' Association. Two decades ago, the Windward Islands supplied 60 per cent of UK bananas; now the Islands' share has plummeted to 9 per cent, displaced by lower-cost bananas from Latin America. Supplying his crops to Sainsbury's and Waitrose, Mr Rene says he thinks fair trade is the only way forward for his industry.

"My local group of 80 members signed up to Fairtrade at an important time. It was at the point when farmers here were thinking of stopping producing bananas; we just couldn't compete. Farmers here get almost double the rate for a box of bananas under Fairtrade and also a $1 premium per box. This has given me some stability to borrow from the bank and I set up a preschool for 34 children in my area.

Individual farmers here pay about 400 Caribbean dollars (£91) per year to be registered and I do think this is a little too much, especially when your production is low and you have high costs.

But, we are more empowered here. We know what is taking place in the market and we have closer links to retailers. They tell us if they have problems and we do whatever we can to try and fix them.

I know I can't only depend on one product and I have diversified into others, but I know my passion, my love and my future is in bananas. For as long as there is a market, I'll be a farmer. Fairtrade is the way forward—it is a way of keeping poor producers like myself earning a living."

But Is It Fair?

Yes: It Puts People Back at the Heart of Trade
By Harriet Lamb, Fairtrade Foundation

Fairtrade does what it says on the tin: it is about better prices for smallholder farmers and workers in developing countries. Fairtrade addresses the injustices of conventional trade, which too often leaves the poorest, weakest producers earning less than it costs them to grow their crops. It's a bit like a national minimum wage for global trade. Not perfect, not a magic want, not a panacea for all the problems of poverty, but a step in the right direction.

Free-market economists complain that Fairtrade benefits only a small number of farmers, penalising those outside. This is plain wrong. In fact, the evidence suggests that the opposite is true. Research in Bolivia, for example, found that coffee producers outside Fairtrade were able to negotiate higher prices: Fairtrade had become a price setter. Fairtrade farmers also share their knowledge in trading. For those inside the system, our research shows that through the minimum price guarantee, farmers have more secure and stable incomes. A group of rice farmers in India invested their premium in buying a tractor and a land leveller; productivity increased by 30 per cent.

Other critics ask why we are working with retailers or big brands like Cadbury's and Starbucks. Our answer is that only by mainstreaming Fairtrade will we be able to reach more producers.

So we are unapologetic in our commitment to scale up. By doing so, moreover, we begin to affect all business behaviour.

A favourite question is why don't we work with UK farmers. We recognise that many farmers in the UK face similar issues to farmers elsewhere, but Fairtrade was established specifically to support the most disadvantaged producers in the world—like the tea-growers of Malawi, who don't even have drinking water in their villages. I always buy my cheese, pears and carrots from my local farmers' market—and enjoy Fairtrade bananas, tea and coffee. It's two sides of the same movement to put people back at the heart of trade. Surely you cannot say fairer than that.

No: Other Schemes Are Just as Valuable
By Philip Booth, Institute of Economic Affairs

Private certification schemes are the unsung heroes of a market economy. They are far more effective than state regulation. It is therefore with a heavy heart that I have always had reservations about Fairtrade-labelled products. The foundation pounces on critics with its well-oiled publicity machine, always responding with anecdotes. But doubts remain.

There are many ways in which poor farmers can get better prices. They can do so through speciality brands, via traditional trade channels and using other labelling initiatives. Does Fairtrade help? The evidence is limited, but even proponents of Fairtrade would argue that only about 50 per cent of the extra money spent by consumers is available to spend on social projects, and others have suggested a figure much closer to zero. No clear evidence has been produced to suggest that farmers themselves actually receive higher prices under Fairtrade.

Fairtrade cannot help all farmers. Some poorer or remote farmers cannot organise and join up; others cannot afford the fees; still others will be working for larger producers who are excluded from many Fairtrade product lines. Against that background,

"Fairtrade absolutism" does not sit well. Fairtrade schools have to do everything possible to stock Fairtrade products—but, what about speciality brands produced by individual farmers? What about Rainforest Alliance products? Are poor producers to be expected to pay the costs involved to join every labelling scheme?

Fairtrade is a brand that promotes itself the way all brands do. As noted, the brand is prominent in schools. It is worrying that its PowerPoint presentation shows graphs of commodity prices that stop in 2001 and graphs of the coffee price relative to the Fairtrade minimum price that stop in 2006. The picture since then tells a different story. This is marketing, not education.

Fairtrade may do some good in some circumstances, but it does not deserve the unique status it claims for itself.

Fair Trade in Agriculture Helps Farmers Improve Their Quality of Life

SourceTrace

SourceTrace is an organization that develops agriculture software designed to help small farmers and encourage sustainable farming practices.

The agricultural sector, as every other sector, is not immune to the distortions of trade; and achieving a balance of profits between the producer, the trader and the retailer has never been an easy task. Consider the everyday products that we consume—coffee, tea and cocoa which is upheld by the labour of hundreds of thousands of farm workers toiling at the bottom of the production system. It is this bottom section of farm workers and smallholder farmers that is most affected whenever systems of trade have spiraled out of control. Ironically, it is these farmers who produce 70 per cent of the world's food, and yet represent 50 percent of the world's hungriest people. Such a distorted supply chain has been the result of price wars triggered by the constant pressure to keep food prices down in the global economic system—taking away from food its true value, and away from its producers, its true economic value.

The scenario in India alone shows that 7.7 million farmers quit agriculture as an occupation since 2001. Coupled with the nearly 27,000 farmer suicides since 1995, the high cost of inputs and limited access to finance, smallholder farmers have become an insecure and poorly paid lot—unfairly so.

Bringing sustainable and dignified living to the smallholder farmer community requires corrections in the supply chain that can be greatly impacted by governments, businesses and investors. Thus, the notion of Fairtrade began with the need for this correction, in Europe in the 1960's. It began as an educative

"Playing It Fair: Fairtrade in Agriculture," SourceTrace. Reprinted by permission.

concept that used alternative trade methods to expose to the European public, the injustice and social imbalance caused by international trade. It revealed that the terms of trade (price relation between raw materials and processed or technical goods) were much in favour of industrialised nations. Fairtrade countered this orientation by developing special criteria for sustainable trade and began implementation of its norms by working with some of "colonialism products" like tea, coffee and cocoa.

Conceptually, Fairtrade is a method of trade that incorporates a long-term perspective and sustainable development for all parties concerned; especially empowering smallholder farmers by addressing some key points such as: Increasing farmers' voice, influence and organization by providing better access to markets, subsidies for inputs such as fuel, seed and machinery, and the opportunity for smallholder farmers to secure land rights. Gain fair value for their products by building supply chains that are fairer—thereby improving farmers' negotiating power and enabling them to build direct business partnerships with retailers. Access to finance: By providing access to finance, smallholder farmers will be able to afford new technology, inputs and diversify their crop base.

Future-proofed farming: Farmers are helped with sustainable practices in order to adapt to the demands of climate change by investing in adaptive technologies. Targeted government spending: At present, developing countries dependent on agriculture spend only around 5 per cent of their national budgets on the sector. This must be increased, while also targeting women farmers who produce 60-80 per cent of the food in most developing countries. Leading and coordinating the Fairtrade movement is the World Fair Trade Organisation (WFTO), a global network of organizations representing the Fair Trade supply chain. Membership with WFTO provides Fairtrade member-organisations with credibility and identity by way of an international guarantee system. WFTO's vision is a world in which trade structures and practices work in favour of the poor, and promote sustainable development and justice.

Ever since Fairtrade as a system of trade came into force, it has set new paradigms such as higher standards of living and reduced risk and vulnerability for farmers and workers. Since the products are safeguarded by a "minimum price" mechanism, it sets a safety net for farmers, which means they are much less affected by price volatility in the market. Secondly, Fairtrade has enabled farmer groups to run stronger businesses through administrative efficiency and better and transparent governance. Thirdly, Fairtrade norms protect farmers' basic rights, providing them with a safe working environment and negotiating power over their wages and working conditions. Fourth, it places demands on the farmers too, requiring them to switch to environmentally-friendly practices.

Fifth, it enables farmers and workers to take control of their businesses, through a tracking mechanism from producer to buyer. Most of all, Fairtrade recognizes the role of women in agriculture, while also keeping its focus on the quality of produce, rather than just quantity. Lastly, the farming community earns a "Fairtrade Premium" over and above the minimum price, which enables farmers and workers to invest in their communities to improve access to basic services. The community can invest this "premium" money where it can have most impact. Studies have shown that this premium is invested in ways as diverse as setting up a dispensary in the community, to paying children's school fees for those who cannot afford it, to setting up kitchen gardens, or even to buy vehicles to reduce cost of transport.

Products that are produced under Fairtrade norms also display the Fairtrade label, which assures consumers that products bearing it meet the Fairtrade Standards. The Fairtrade Mark indicates that the product has been certified to give a better deal to the producers involved while also protecting the environment. Fairtrade is being set up in India now because Indian producers have long been involved in the Fairtrade movement, exporting their products to consumers in Europe and North America and getting better prices and terms of trade. Building on this success, while facing agrarian crisis at home, local producers in India identified an opportunity to connect with their own markets, thus strengthening production and food security.

There are signs that smallholder agriculture is starting to be recognized as a potential powerhouse to fix a broken system, including the launch by G8 world leaders of the New Alliance for Food Security and Nutrition—an agreement that comprises country-specific commitments codified in what is called "Cooperation Frameworks." However, the international Fairtrade system argues that overall financial investment required to mainstream Fairtrade practices remains inadequate. With governments increasingly focusing on the role of multinational companies and agribusiness, Fairtrade argues that policymakers are missing the potential solutions that could be delivered by smallholder farmer organisations themselves as key agents for food security, rural economic development, and, for some, trading relations that lift communities out of poverty. Despite all that, the uplifting results achieved by the Fairtrade movement so far can hardly be undermined.

Fair Trade Supports Producers and Their Communities Socially, Environmentally, and Economically

Friends of the Earth Limited

Friends of the Earth Limited is a UK-based volunteer organization that unites local groups for environmental grassroots campaigns.

How does Fairtrade work and what are the advantages? Here are just some of the benefits of buying Fairtrade.

Why Buy Fairtrade?

There are currently millions of hardworking farmers in developing countries—producing the food that ends up in our shopping baskets—that are not being paid enough to support their families.

If we buy food products without thinking where they come from or who produced it we become part of the problem by feeding exploitation.

But by choosing Fairtrade products farmers get a better deal and a more stable income so that they can feed, educate and take care of their children.

When farmers sell their crops via Fairtrade cooperatives and plantations, they get more money to invest back into better farming methods, clean water and improving the health of their communities.

What Does the Fairtrade Mark Mean?

Fairtrade International is the most widely-recognised ethical label in the world.

The Mark means the product's ingredients have been produced by small-scale farmer organisations that meet Fairtrade's social, economic and environmental standards.

"The Benefits of Fairtrade," Friends of the Earth Limited, March 2, 2017. Reprinted by permission.

These standards include protection of the environment, workers' rights and the payment of the Fairtrade Minimum Price and an additional Fairtrade Premium to invest in business or community projects.

The aim is to use trade, not aid, to help small-scale farmers; one of the most marginalised groups in the world.

Fairtrade Facts and Figures

- There are 1.65 million farmers and workers in Fairtrade certified producer organisations.
- There are a total of 1,226 Fairtrade producer organisations in 74 countries.
- A quarter of all workers in Fairtrade are women.
- Farmer and worker organisations own 50% of the global Fairtrade system.
- On plantations, 26% of workers spent their Fairtrade premiums on education.
- The Fairtrade foods sold in the biggest quantities worldwide are bananas, coffee beans, sugar and cocoa beans.
- However other Fairtrade products include wine, tea, cotton, flowers, rice, orange juice and gold.

Fairtrade Means Fair Wages for Farmers

For most Fairtrade goods there is a Fairtrade minimum price which acts as an important safety net, protecting farmers from fluctuating market prices. This ensures farmers can earn and expect a stable income and plan for their future.

Fairtrade is the only certification scheme that offers such a unique minimum price protection for farmers.

In addition, a Fairtrade Premium is also paid into a communal fund for workers and farmers to use as they see fit—this could be on education or healthcare for their children, improving their business or building infrastructure such as roads and bridges for their community.

Fairtrade Is Fairer for the Environment

To be Fairtrade certified organisations must conform to rigorous environmental standards.

Farmers are encouraged to move towards organic production and:

- Protect their local environment through minimal and safe use of agrochemicals.
- Manage erosion problems and waste management properly.
- Maintain soil fertility.
- Avoid intentionally using genetically modified organisms (GMOs).
- Continually monitor the impact they have on the environment and implement ways to keep on reducing it.

Fairtrade Coffee Benefits Farmers and Communities

Coffee farmers in Costa Rica have invested in ovens fuelled by the discarded coffee husks of the very beans they are roasting.

This has reduced the number of trees cut down for firewood.

The Nicaraguan UCA cooperative has built a pre-school using the premium earned from its coffee.

Fairtrade Bans Child Labour

Fairtrade means zero-tolerance of child labour, and the organisation works to bring an end to such practices.

Children under 18 years old are banned from work that endangers them or their schooling. And children under 15 are not to be employed by Fairtrade organisations.

More Fairtrade Benefits

- Fairtrade provides access to, and oversees, loans to help producers invest. For example the UCA cooperative took out a loan to construct a drying mill for its coffee. The mill is now paying back the loan that built it and reducing processing costs.

- Fairtrade can improve food security which is closely linked to economic growth, stable incomes and reduced risk and vulnerability. If a farmer has a better income it means he or she has more money to buy food and more money to invest in growing more crops.
- Fairtrade gives shoppers the opportunity to live and shop according to their principles and take action to support farmers and their families.
- Fairtrade provides consumers with an opportunity to connect with the people who grow the produce we enjoy and need.

Did You Know?

- There are 4,500 Fairtrade certified products for sale in the UK, so it's well worth shopping around.
- In 2016, the UK spent £1.64 bn on Fairtrade produce as Fairtrade bananas and coffee rose in popularity.
- Ecuador and Costa Rica traditionally earn around 9 and 8 per cent respectively of their total export earnings from bananas alone.
- In 2015 more than half (55%) of Fairtrade bananas sold were organic, as were 59% of all Fairtrade coffee beans.

Does Fair Trade Help the Poor, or Just Relieve Guilt?

Hugh Outhred and Maria Retnanestri

Hugh Outhred is a senior visiting fellow at the University of New South Wales in Australia and has served as an energy advisor for governments and corporations alike. Maria Retnanestri is a visiting research fellow at the University of New South Wales. Her research focuses on the sustainability of renewable energy projects.

That "fair trade" sticker on a bar of chocolate or bag of coffee beans might make you feel better, but there's no guarantee it's helping poor farmers. In fact, it may be making their lives worse.

When people make decisions they usually have an intended consequence in mind, based on their mental models of how the world works. Unfortunately our mental models may not fully represent the real world.

What's more, most of our decisions have unintended consequences that may detract from the intended outcome. This problem arises with "fair trade."

The Fair Trade Advocacy Office provides a Fair Trade definition.

It says: "Fair Trade is a trading partnership, based on dialogue, transparency and respect, that seeks greater equity in international trade. It contributes to sustainable development by offering better trading conditions to, and securing the rights of, marginalized producers and workers—especially in the South.

"Fair Trade Organizations, backed by consumers, are engaged actively in supporting producers, awareness raising and in campaigning for changes in the rules and practice of conventional international trade."

On the same web site, the Charter of Fair Trade Principles provides the following motivation for fair trade:

"Fair Trade … is, fundamentally, a response to the failure of conventional trade to deliver sustainable livelihoods and development opportunities to people in the poorest countries of the world; this is evidenced by the two billion of our fellow citizens who, despite working extremely hard, survive on less than $2 per day."

Is Fair Trade Setting Itself Up to Fail?

In principle, fair trade's product certification allows a conscientious consumer to choose a product or service that will support a sustainable livelihood in a poor country.

Unfortunately, it is at this step that questions arise. Rather than addressing the underlying causes of human inequality, "fair trade" operates via a fragile change to conventional trade. The Charter says conventional trade fails "to deliver sustainable livelihoods and development opportunities to people in the poorest countries of the world."

The fragility arises because of a perverse incentive: participating organisations have to capture the benefits of product certification while minimising the costs of doing so.

As a result, the scheme requires intensive regulation by "certifiers." They have to avoid two types of unintended consequence—developed world consumers lose confidence and stop participating in the scheme, or they continue to pay higher prices for certified products but "middle men" siphon off the additional cash.

From this perspective, the certifiers are, of course, merely one category of "middle men." There is no escape from the unintended consequence that intermediaries will capture at least a fraction of the discretionary cash flow intended for poor producers.

The remaining issues are how large this "overhead" will be and which intermediaries capture most of it.

Another potential unintended consequence is that producers in poor countries will stop producing traditional crops for local consumption. Instead, they will switch to "cash crops" that are attractive to "fair trade" consumers in rich countries but detract from human welfare in their home country.

Certification Doesn't See the Big Picture

The concept of food value chains (FVCs) can help explain the problems with fair trade. A recent Science Forum article defines FVCs as "all activities required to bring farm products to consumers, including agricultural production, processing, storage, marketing, distribution and consumption."

This definition illustrates the "fair trade" challenge. The target group, "marginalised producers and workers—especially in the south," is only a small link in the chain that brings products to consumers in developed countries.

Some of the products that are going to developed country consumers may have been diverted from poor country consumers that need them. In some cases, the chains set up to bring us "fair trade" products may have completely displaced chains that distribute products in poorer countries.

The people involved in a food value chain are a social system. The system may be a civic network characterised by mutual respect and reciprocity. It may be a social field characterised by social competition.

Human inequality is a clear indication that human society as a global whole is better characterised as a social field than a civic network. It appears unlikely that "fair trade" will change that.

Is There a Better Way to Support Small Farmers?

Research Principles for Developing Country Food Chains suggests a more holistic approach to supporting small farmers in poor countries:

1. Focus on opportunities in domestic markets: we should help poor countries improve their internal food value chains.

2. Enhance marketing channel efficiency: we should make sure that chains in poor countries are as efficient as possible. This can stop prices in poor countries from becoming artificially high.

3. Pay attention to indirect effects, not only to increased sales from smallholders: we should try to improve the lot of poor farmers and workers in a more holistic fashion.

4. Pay attention to post-harvest losses, both in volume and quality: these losses directly reduce the nutrition available to people in poor countries.

5. Help small farmers conserve natural resources: improved productivity can reduce the impact of food production on natural ecosystems.

6. Go beyond certification: certification can be costly and exclude smallholder farmers from high-value markets. It may not promote adoption of sustainable farming practices or foster farm-level innovation.

Apart from the above principles, it is clear that in our ever more crowded and constrained global village, we should all live as prudently as possible.

Multinational Corporations Pose a Danger to Small Fair Trade Producers

Agatha Herman

Agatha Herman is a lecturer at Cardiff University in Wales who specializes in human geography.

Fairtrade products and promotions are covered with photos of smiling producers, but behind the marketing gloss not everyone is so happy.

Becoming a Fairtrade producer—and maintaining required standards—can be complex and ambiguous, with continual market and organisational challenges. And, since Fairtrade started to allow major multinational corporations—including Nestlé and Starbucks—to join in recent years, producers are beginning to question the scheme's aims.

For the past two years, I have been working with Fairtrade wine producer communities in Argentina, Chile and South Africa. While I found they recognise the benefits of being associated with Fairtrade, there are downsides that consumers often do not know about.

Set up more than 20 years ago, Fairtrade International positions itself as a connector between disadvantaged producers in developing countries and consumers, building and supporting strong, direct and long-term relationships.

Nearly 80% of UK consumers recognise the Fairtrade mark. With many big supermarkets now involved, sales—of things like bananas, coffee and sugar—are growing every year.

Across the world, 1.65 million farmers and workers—totalling 1,226 "producer organisations"—are Fairtrade certified and display the Fairtrade mark on products.

"Why Small Producers Have Big Concerns about Multinationals Joining Fairtrade," by Agatha Herman, The Conversation, May 11, 2017. https://theconversation.com/why-small-producers-have-big-concerns-about-multinationals-joining-fairtrade-73734. Licensed under CC BY 4.0 International.

For small producers and workers, Fairtrade offers huge opportunities far beyond just selling produce. Farmworkers' communities in the Western Cape, South Africa, for example, have also benefited from improved education, physical and mental health care, community interaction and housing.

Some workers also talk of better relations with their white owner-managers, though for others the legacies of apartheid have proved more persistent. But, from my findings, it seems that the longer a farm has been Fairtrade the more likely it is that traditional worker-owner relations are challenged.

High Standards

For the small grape producers of Argentina and Chile, Fairtrade has been a lifeline in a market dominated by large multinational corporations. "If we lost Fairtrade … I would die as a producer, it is not profitable," one Chilean producer told me.

In 1997, when this producer's association was first approached by an European Fairtrade organisation, they couldn't believe their luck in terms of the prices they were offered. As the producer remembered: "…in those years we produced 20,000 kilos per hectare. Then we said 'if the gringos pay so well, we'll continue producing at those levels.'

"It turned out in 2001 that our wine was bad … they told us 'if you improve, we continue buying. If not, no.' From there, we transformed completely…"

Understandably, Fairtrade has high standards to maintain. Now the association grows fewer, higher quality grapes in more environmentally friendly ways, resulting in better wine. This is one of Fairtrade's key benefits: it helps producers understand exactly what consumers want.

Level Playing Field?

But these benefits do not come easy. In Argentina and Chile, small producers are struggling with large corporations joining the Fairtrade system. Though these brands buy Fairtrade ingredients—a win for farmers—producers are now competing for certified shelf space with multinationals. Another small Chilean producer told me:

> Every day there is more competition … the big companies certify, in the case of wine in Chile like Concha y Toro, like Cono Sur, like Miguel Torres. They have everything cheaper because they have wineries bottling plants, specialised people selling … it is very difficult to compete and the doors are closing.

Tensions are rising—and producers are questioning who Fairtrade should support. It was established as the champion of small producers but as the market has grown it has become more attractive to big companies—and Fairtrade is letting them join. The manager of a Chilean producer association told me in 2016:

> Do you think that Concha y Toro deserves to be so privileged in this market? No … that is not why Fairtrade was invented.

The entrance of big companies is having serious knock-on effects that could undo any boosts to small producers. One boutique winery in Argentina is no longer able to support the Fairtrade association of small producers it helped to establish because it cannot compete with multinationals' low prices. More generally, South America's small producers are overwhelmed by the paperwork involved and struggle with the business expertise and language skills needed.

South African farmer-owners are also frustrated by the minefield of ever-changing regulations. One questioned Fairtrade regulators' experience in farming and business, adding: "…whatever they think would be nice to put in, they put in not realising what the implications are."

Partnerships

When told of the producers' concerns, Sarah Singer, Fairtrade Foundation supply chain manager, said: "Working with big companies and supporting small producers and workers is not mutually exclusive. Fairtrade exists to challenge the inequalities and power imbalances in trade so that farmers and workers from developing countries get a better deal.

"We work in partnership with farmers and workers, they co-own our system and it is they who decide whether to work with bigger companies. They are often keen to do so because this creates more opportunities to sell greater volumes of their produce, at higher prices and the security of longer-term business relationships which means they can invest in improvements to their farms and their communities."

For the small farmers of South America who have seen their non-Fairtrade neighbours uprooting vineyards to sell to developers and for workers in South Africa, Argentina and Chile who are experiencing community development, Fairtrade remains a good opportunity. But—despite Fairtrade's assurances—whether only small producers and workers should be supported and how, or if there is a place for big companies too, requires further discussion and better communication.

Organizations to Contact

The editors have compiled the following list of organizations concerned with the issues debated in this book. The descriptions are derived from materials provided by the organizations. All have publications or information available for interested readers. This list was compiled on the date of publication of the present volume; the information provided here may change. Be aware that many organizations take several weeks or longer to respond to inquiries, so allow as much time as possible.

Amnesty International
5 Penn Plaza, 16th Floor
New York, NY 10001
phone: (212) 807-8400
website: www.amnestyusa.org

Amnesty International is a global human rights organization that aims to stop human rights violations through research, mobilization, and advocacy. They are dedicated to a number of issues, from protecting refugee rights to ensuring gender and identity equality. Their principles focus on fairness under the law around the world, whether that's related to fair working conditions and wages or freedom of expression. They have several issue-based publications available to read online.

Brookings Institution
1775 Massachusetts Avenue NW
Washington, DC 20036
phone: (202) 797-6000
email: communications@brookings.edu
website: www.brookings.edu

The Brookings Institution is a nonprofit public policy organization that conducts independent research. The Brookings Institution uses its research to provide recommendations that advance the goals of strengthening American democracy, fostering social welfare and security, and securing a cooperative international system. The organization publishes a variety of books, reports, and commentary that deal with the issue of how to approach trade.

Cato Institute
1000 Massachusetts Avenue NW
Washington, DC 20001-5403
phone: (202) 842-0200
website: www.cato.org

The Cato Institute is a public policy research organization dedicated to the principles of individual liberty, limited government, free markets, and peace. The Cato Institute aims to provide clear, thoughtful, and independent analysis on vital public policy issues. The Institute publishes numerous policy studies, two quarterly journals—*Regulation* and *Cato Journal*—and the bimonthly *Cato Policy Report*.

Fair Trade Federation
100 W. 10th Street, Suite 604
Wilmington, DE 19801
phone: (302) 655-5203
email: info@fairtradefederation.org
website: www.fairtradefederation.org

The Fair Trade Federation is an organization of Canadian and American businesses that choose to practice fair trade. Their goals are justice, sustainability, community empowerment, and partnership. Additionally, they stress the importance of consumer choice that comes with the knowledge of how their purchases affect the world around them. The Fair Trade Federation is part of the international fair trade network.

Fair Trade USA
1500 Broadway, Suite 400
Oakland, CA 94612
phone: (510) 663-5260
website: www.fairtradecertified.org

Fair Trade USA is part of the global fair trade network. It promotes sustainability and local growth through a trade network that puts communities and the planet first. Their guiding principle is that trade must incorporate ethics. Through fair trade they allow consumers the ability to select products that help increase equality around the world.

The Organization for Economic Co-operation and Development (OECD)
OECD Washington Center
1776 I Street NW, Suite 450
Washington, DC 20006
phone: (202) 785-6323
email: washington.contact@oecd.org
website: www.oecd.org/unitedstates

The Organization for Economic Co-operation and Development is an international group that seeks to enhance trade relations and economic development between partner members. Member countries are limited to democracies with a market economy. Their current goals include shaping policies that promote economic growth while considering equality and opportunity for citizens.

Rainforest Alliance
125 Broad Street, 9th Floor
New York, NY 10004
phone: (212) 677-1900
email: info@ra.org
website: www.rainforest-alliance.org

The Rainforest Alliance is a nonprofit organization and group of businesses, communities, and consumers that prioritize social and environmental issues in conjunction with business endeavors. Their goal is to conserve biodiversity, protect the environment, and promote more sustainable practices. They publish online reports about climate change, deforestation, and other ecological threats.

The World Fair Trade Organization (WFTO)
Godfried Bomansstraat 8-3
4103 WR Culemborg
The Netherlands
phone: +31 (0) 345 53 64 87
website: www.wfto.com

The World Fair Trade Organization consists of members around the globe that practice fair trade. The organization focuses on promoting both fair trade and social enterprise by putting people and the environment first. Members must be verified by the organization as complying with fair trade standards. The WFTO has a podcast and regularly publishes articles online.

The World Trade Organization (WTO)
Centre William Rappard
Rue de Lausanne, 154
Case postale, 1211 Genève 2
Switzerland
phone : +41 (0)22 739 51 11
email: enquiries@wto.org
website: www.wto.org/index.htm

The World Trade Organization is an international and intergovernmental trade association. Their goal is to reduce barriers to trade around the world and help nations and companies conduct their business. The WTO also helps settle international trade disputes. They release annual reports on trade and their internal operations.

Bibliography

Books

John Bowes, *The Fair Trade Revolution*. London, UK: Pluto, 2011.

Keith R. Brown, *Buying into Fair Trade: Culture, Morality, and Consumption*. New York, NY: New York University Press, 2013.

Jacqueline DeCarlo, *Fair Trade: A Beginners Guide*. London, UK: Oneworld, 2010.

I. Hudson and M. Fridell, *Fair Trade, Sustainability, and Social Change*. Basingstoke, UK: Palgrave Macmillan UK, 2013.

Anna Hutchens, *Changing Big Business: The Globalisation of the Fair Trade Movement*. Cheltenham, UK: Edward Elgar Publishing, 2010.

Daniel Jaffee, *Brewing Justice: Fair Trade Coffee, Sustainability, and Survival*. Berkeley, CA: University of California Press, 2014.

Harriet Lamb, *Fighting the Banana Wars and Other Fairtrade Battles*. London, UK: Rider, 2009.

Mary Ann Littrell and Marsha Ann Dickson, *Artisans and Fair Trade: Crafting Development*. Sterling, VA: Kumarian Press, 2010.

Sarah Lyon and Mark Moberg, *Fair Trade and Social Justice: Global Ethnographies*. New York, NY: New York University Press, 2010.

Mark Pendergrast. *Beyond Fair Trade: How One Small Coffee Company Helped Transform a Hillside Village in Thailand*. Vancouver, BC: Greystone Books, 2015.

Laura T. Raynolds, *The Challenges of Transforming Globalization.* London, UK: Routledge, 2007.

Laura T. Raynolds and Elizabeth A. Bennett, *Handbook of Research on Fair Trade.* Cheltenham, UK: Edward Elgar Publishing, 2016.

Ruerd Ruben, *The Impact of Fair Trade.* Wageningen, NL: Wageningen Academic Publishers, 2009.

Ndongo Samba Sylla and David Clément Leye, *The Fair Trade Scandal: Marketing Poverty to Benefit the Rich.* London, UK: Pluto Press, 2014.

E. Valiente-Riedl, *Is Fairtrade Fair?* Basingstoke, UK: Palgrave Macmillan UK. 2013.

Meera Warrier. *The Politics of Fair Trade: A Survey.* London, UK: Routledge, 2014.

Conor Woodman. *Unfair Trade.* New York, NY: Random House Business, 2014.

Periodicals and Internet Sources

Nasser Abufarha, "How Do You Know It's Really Fair Trade?" Fair World Project. fairworldproject.org/validation-programs.

Jèrôme Ballet and Aurèlie Carimentrand, "Fair Trade and the Depersonalization of Ethics," *Journal of Business Ethics,* 2010. www.jstor.org/stable/27919145.

Michael Barratt Brown, "'Fair Trade' with Africa," *Review of African Political Economy,* 2007. https://doi.org/10.1080/03056240701449653.

Raluca Dragusanu et al., "The Economics of Fair Trade," *Journal of Economic Perspectives,* 2014. www.jstor.org/stable/23800584.

Colleen Height. "The Problem with Fair Trade Coffee," *Stanford Social Innovation Review: Informing and Inspiring Leaders of Social Change*, Summer 2011. ssir.org/articles/entry/the_problem_with_fair_trade_coffee.

Anna Hutchens. "Empowering Women Through Fair Trade? Lessons from Asia," *Third World Quarterly*, 2010. www.jstor.org/stable/27867935.

Geoff Moore. "The Fair Trade Movement: Parameters, Issues and Future Research," *Journal of Business Ethics*, 2004. www.jstor.org/stable/25123283.

Amy Shoenthal. "What Exactly Is Fair Trade, and Why Should We Care?" *Forbes*, December 14, 2018. www.forbes.com/sites/amyschoenberger/2018/12/14/what-exactly-is-fair-trade-and-why-should-we-care/#450717297894.

Andrew Walton. "What Is Fair Trade?" *Third World Quarterly*, 2010. www.jstor.org/stable/27867934.

Index

5